What readers are saying about *Wine, Women, Whispers* By Alon Mintz, a.k.a. Rocky Mintziano, Adam Savage, Ali Mintez...

"*Wine, Women, Whispers* is about a quirky and very interesting man of the world. He got his wanderlust from his father, who issued him an edict — to study at many schools, and travel to many countries in order to become all he could be. In fact both parents were unique, insisting the author not pigeonhole himself into a career prematurely; they inspired him instead to do wonderful things with his life. I loved the homage to his mother, which is very tender. The book is a fast read that makes you want to know more about the author — whether he is called Alon Mintz (his given name), Rocky Mintziano, Adam Savage, Adam Stephens, or Ali Mintz. His crazy and not so crazy escapades are fun to read, and make me kind of envious that I haven't done half the things he has in his lifetime."
Susan Pinkus, Former Director
Los Angeles Times Public Opinion Polls

"*Wine, Women, Whispers* is written in an easy to follow and captivating fashion. I like the stories, which seem almost surreal at times. They captured my interest because they take place in an international arena. I, too, have lived in or traveled to a number of places in the book, and it was intriguing to revisit them through the author's perspective."
Moty Zahavi. writer, actor, former Israeli soldier

"Riveting!"
Kathy Aaronson, President, Sales Athlete Executive Search

WINE, WOMEN, WHISPERS

Alon Mintz

Edited by Ina Hillebrandt
Cover design by Ina Hillebrandt, with Carolyn Allen
Cover photo by Jerry Maybrook
Book design by Ina Hillebrandt

Published in the United States of America by Pawpress
Brentwood Village • PO Box 492213
Los Angeles, CA 90049

Library of Congress Control Number: 2010926660

ISBN 978-1-880882-14-6

a PAWPRESS book
InasPawprints.com

Published by Lightning Source, on acid-free paper, from pulp of non-endangered species, non-old growth trees.

WINE, WOMEN, WHISPERS

ALON MINTZ, a.k.a.

Rocky Mintziano, Adam Savage, Ali Mintez ...

Edited by Ina Hillebrandt

I dedicate this book to my incredible wife Carol, who is my rock and true foundation. If she had not given me the wonderful birthday present of a course in writing memoirs, I question if this work would ever have been accomplished.

PREFACE

Carol's amazing present to me was this: she paid $90.00 for me to attend a UCLA course on writing your autobiography. It was one of the things I always "intended" to do. As years passed, I honestly don't know exactly what it was — a challenge, ego, the desire to actually do it — but I went determined to do my best. The classes were broken into small groups of four or five adults. I use the word adults as everyone there was supposed to be at least 60 years of age, so as to have lived a long life, and have stories to relate that they were finally prepared to share with others.

In my case, I wanted my sharing to be with friends and my growing family. To let them know who I was. What kind of person. Where I lived in my 70 years. When and where I worked. And the good times and not so pleasant ones. To try to recall moments that were in numerous cases very long ago. It may not be a simple task, and I may not get all the t's crossed or i's dotted, but I'll do my best. I hope you find the stories interesting, and in most cases enjoyable.

One of the difficulties in writing this memoir is that I cannot include everything that has come my way. There have to be some limitations for personal reasons, and of course for readers' sakes! In the hopes that my family's children will have a chance to read what I've written, I have edited out the "naughty" bits. Sorry!

ACKNOWLEDGEMENTS

I still revel over the day of my first class at UCLA. Of about twenty people who showed up, there are only three of us still writing: Tomi Fields, Alice Lewis and me. We have met almost every week and supported each other. They are wonderful writers whose own stories I have never tired of hearing. Without them, I don't know if I would ever have gone on to recall so much of my past. I look forward to seeing their stories in print and insist on autographed copies!

Finally, I would like to thank my editor, Ina Hillebrandt. Without her help completing this book would not have been possible.

Alon Mintz, a.k.a. Rocky, 2010

Editor's Note

One of the reasons I elected to take on this project is the character and person who is Alon Mintz, or Rocky, depending. His tales are not only captivating, they are the stories of a fearless man. Seeing how he turns every challenge into an opportunity has made working with Alon a constant delight, and a reminder of the importance of living life to the hilt.

Ina Hillebrandt

TABLE OF CONTENTS

BY WAY OF INTRODUCTION

One point that stands out in my life is my father's very serious talk with me, before he passed away. I had worked summers at his shoe stores, understood the business, and would have grown it even more. But one day when we were alone, he informed me that he was selling the company to an investor. I was extremely surprised and said so. His answer was the best I could have hoped for. "The funds will all go to your mother, who will spend them on you, your younger brother and herself. They might last two, perhaps even four years. After that I expect you to look after her the rest of her life. If she remarries, that's fine as long as he's a good, caring man that the three of you like. As for you, I have other plans that I can only hope will come to fruition. I think that for some reason you're a little different from most of the young men I've come in contact with. Not better or worse, just different."

He continued, "There were many things I wanted to do with my life, especially to travel and study. Meeting people from different backgrounds would have been fascinating. I'm suggesting that when I'm gone and your mother and Steve are settled, you leave not only the city but perhaps the country. You need not go to one school, go to a number of them. Experience different places, ideas, foods, religions, colors, and new progressive thoughts that will spur you on to do things that I can hardly dream about. Where you will end your journey, I have no idea. That's exciting, the way life should be."

After he passed away, I related his message to Mom and my brother Steve. They both were totally supportive. I like to think he'd be pleased with the way things turned out.

FAMILY

"Pops" Josephson

MY PARENTS
DAD

When my father died of a heart problem — that today could be fixed on an outpatient basis — I was only seventeen. I had adored Dad and missed him terribly. To me he looked like the actor Rudolph Valentino. He had a fine singing voice, and on occasion even crooned with Eddie Fisher. He was a complete gentleman, and although I saw the ladies give him the eye, he was a great husband and father.

My younger brother Steve and I were extremely lucky to have had the Dad we did. He was handsome, bright, had a marvelous sense of humor, attended any events that we participated in. The time we got to spend with him was always joyous, and he was a terrific role model for us as well. Mom adored him and never remarried. He was fabulous to her and to people in general. For example, I remember a time when a man said "Damn!" in front of my mother. Dad immediately reprimanded the fellow. "Don't you use words like that when my wife is in the room!" The man protested, "But it's only 'damn.' It's in the Bible!" My father was quite insistent, though — no bad language in front of his wife. It was a powerful lesson for me, one which has stayed with me all of my life.

Dad owned shoe stores in different sections of Philadelphia. Any fireman or policeman could purchase shoes for their families at a major discount. That turned out to be a big help to me anytime I got into trouble — like if I were speeding and got pulled over, the policeman would look at my license and say, "Mintz? Is your father Lee, the shoe man?" And when I'd answer, "Yes," they'd say, "OK. I'll let you go this time. But drive a little slower."

MOM

My Mother Anne was eighty-one when she died. Mom was diagnosed with cancer in her early forties and told that she probably wouldn't have more than a few years. She was a hell of a broad, and told them they didn't know what they were talking about. Over the years, they removed various parts of her body. She had a double mastectomy, lost other parts of her body.

But she was totally with it. I remember when she told me, "These doctors don't know me. I want to see what my boys grow up to be."

She was a big shock to the medical practitioners, a woman who could outlive their predictions, and by a good forty years. But she was strong and strong-willed. When she was in her sixties, she visited me in my home in Mill Valley, in Northern California. We went for a drive one day and most of the conversation was about death, and her passing. I informed her that her passing was quite an impossibility at that time. I was moving to Europe and would certainly need her wisdom and strength as a young man just beginning my journeys to foreign lands.

Subsequently, we both had the joy of her visiting me in many countries. She was a fantastic traveling companion and very wise. I was fortunate to have her with me during many of my business and personal encounters.

I remember we were Norway, in the land of the midnight sun, and she sat alongside me and rowed the boat. And many times during this and later trips, if I spotted a lady I might be interested in somewhere, she'd say, "You go for it! We have two rooms. Have a good evening. I'll see you tomorrow."

There were only two women my mom disapproved of. One was Sherry, an actress I dated for a short time. I had to go to Cedars

Sinai hospital for a back operation and Sherry came to see me. She was sitting on my bed, just kind of playing with me, partially undressed, when my mother came in. You would have thought she would straighten herself out, but she didn't. There was no respect.

Mom said, "She's not for you. Too crass. No class."

Mom was right. I remember Sherry had to have an abortion (not my child), and she went to a clinic for it. After it was completed and she and a friend were walking out, they were roughed up by a couple of guys. One grabbed Sherry by the throat. She pulled out her purse and took out a derringer, shooting the ring leader. Without looking back, she and her friend proceeded to their car and drove home. One tough lady.

Sharon was the other woman my mother didn't approve of. I must have dated 50 women like Sharon — like Susan, Sherry, any name that began with an "s." For some reason, if there's an "s" in front of their name, they were mine. Sharon was a fashion model. She had a figure to die for, and no hesitation in showing it. We hit it off great, even though she wasn't the brightest bulb in the chandelier. Actually, like many English women of that time, she didn't have much education — had completed school only up to the eighth grade. But she was a nice person, uncomplicated. I was running a new business and she was right for me at the time.

Mom tried to have conversations with her, but rarely succeeded. She gave me the hint that this is not the one for you. Sharon went on a shoot, met a count or a duke or something, and he swept her away to his own country. Within a short time she was married and pregnant. Once again, Mom was right.

But one of the most important "being rights" was yet to come…

BROTHER STEVE

When my father died I had to become the man of the house at the age of seventeen and a half, as the eldest of the two children. This was something I felt ready to do. We were living in Florida when we lost him. I started my grown-up role by arranging for his body to be shipped back to Philadelphia, where he was to be buried in the family plot. Next, I felt it was my responsibility to make sure the daily tasks of life were taken care of — paying important bills on time, making sure the car was in proper working order, food was in the refrigerator. These tasks would have been too much for my brother Steve, I felt. He was only fourteen. And he was going through a big growth spurt, which in itself took a lot of his energy and attention: he went from 5'2" to 6' in less than two years.

At this time, Steve was developing as a player of sports. He became a fine athlete, and it is tragic that our father did not have the opportunity to see him excel on the field. Among other athletic achievements, my brother became a great quarterback at Overbrook High. One fun moment still stands out in my mind. I saw him being hit illegally by some members of the other team. In street clothes I jumped over the barrier, ran onto the field, and tried to fight them. I was summarily tossed out of the stadium. My brother asked, "Why did you do that?"

"They were beating you up!" I shot back. The truth is, he was my younger brother and I always felt I should take care of him. Even when guys were a lot bigger than I was I would go after them if I saw them going after Steve. He would say, "Would you stop that! I can take care of myself." And he could take care of himself. There was one time when some guys pulled out a gun and he chased them, got the gun and became a hero. But he was still my little brother, and I still jumped in to protect him, and he still told me to "Stop that!"

ABOUT GRANDPARENTS

Sadly, we had very little contact with my father's parents, and I don't know much about them. As a baby I met both, but they passed away when I was only about 5 years old or so. Time passed and there was little if any mention of them. All we knew was that they were just two people who came from "the Old Country," the Ukraine. He was Alexander. She was Ida. In a census taken in January of 1920, the report stated that he was 38 and she 29. It also said that they had two children, Ruth who was 10, and my Dad, Leon, who was 7. Jeannie was born a few years later. Neither my brother Steve nor I recall Dad speaking of his parents. Today I find it odd that we know so little of them. Perhaps it was that era. The only other reasons I can think of are that they weren't happy together, and that they lived a distance from us.

No one else in the family can tell me anything more than these bare bones about my father's parents. I do recall one more snippet relating to them. My mother, father and brother and I were in Miami getting off a cruise ship once, and there was an elderly couple there who knew my father's parents quite well, and spoke highly of them.

In contrast, I remember clearly and with great affection my mother's mom and dad. As young kids, four and seven years old, Steve and I would go with our parents to their house on Delancey St., where our grandfather Morris, whom we called "Pops," made his own wine.

Once he had just gotten a delivery of grapes and had them all placed in a round open wood tub. That's when he and Dad told Steve and me to take our trousers off. We did, so that we were in our underwear. They said, "Go on, boys, step on those grapes and turn them into juice." We both climbed in, and leaping and jumping about, did our best to try and squash every grape. Our toes and feet were stained red and we were ecstatic with our success. Mother and Grandmom were there with soap and water, and soon we could put our trousers back on and walk on the carpets again. I think that was the first time I ever drank wine. Needless to say, this is one of my favorite childhood memories.

Our grandfather would do his own bottling and had shelves filled with homemade wine. When friends came over he enjoyed sharing the fruits of his (and our) labors. Pop was so proud of his wine he wanted us boys to have a taste, and would put a little bit in a glass of water for my brother and me. We would sit at the kitchen table. Rose, our grandmother, would bring out nibbles like pieces of challah, cookies, and humentasch at the right time of year — she was a great cook and also liked to bake.

Pop was a strapping man with red hair. He was tough as nails, warm as a quilt. Very masculine, but with a great sense of humor. I remember he was good looking, with a shock of red hair before he lost it. Most of my life I was blond, and we were the only two people in our family who never had dark hair. He rented out a whole street and sold Christmas trees in winter, and later the lights and fixings for them. In the summer he sold watermelons. He sold more Christmas trees in winter and watermelons in the summer than anyone. That's all he needed to do. He was quite successful financially just doing those two things, being the biggest watermelon and Christmas tree merchant in Philadelphia.

I remember one time there was a man who came in to buy a tree, and my father recognized him. It was Connie Mack, the owner of the Philadelphia Athletics baseball team. He gave my grandfather tickets and we got to go to the New York Yankees-Philadelphia A's game. Babe Ruth broke a bat, and my father asked if we could have the two halves. The Babe, Lou Gehrig and at least a dozen other players signed that bat. We put a nail in it to keep it together. We got a ball that was signed by these guys, too.

There was a time when I was around 13 or 14, I was in my grandparents' bedroom, and opened up a drawer to see what was inside. I saw a loaded revolver. I was very excited and took it out, and began to practice different shooting positions in front of the mirror. I got lucky. As I was aiming at an imaginary bad guy, I heard footsteps coming up the stairs. There was no time to replace the gun in the drawer without making a lot of noise. So I stashed it in the top of my pants, and managed to close the drawer quietly, just in time. My grandfather had come to fetch me; we were all going out to dinner. I had to wear the gun between my legs the whole time. I kept hoping some bad guy would come in and try to hold up the place, so I could whip out the pistol and be the hero. It was probably a good thing Al Capone never showed up. Heaven knows what would have happened to my private parts.

I told that story to my Mother years later and she smiled and said she recalled the night, as they all thought something was amiss. She then told me that Pop only had blanks in his gun, as he could never bring himself to shoot another person. We both had a good laugh. However, after my grandfather passed away, when I asked if I could have that revolver, my mother saw to it that I never got ahold of it again.

A LITTLE BIT ABOUT MY FATHER'S SISTERS: AUNTS RUTH AND JEANNIE

Aunt Ruth

Aunt Ruth left home at sixteen and moved to Michigan by herself. She had a presence about her that stood out. She was tall, with a fine figure, and wore her black hair tightly pulled back into a bun of sorts. Attractive, she could have passed as a Spanish lady of the Villa. She apparently worked hard and had a keen eye for women's styles. Later a major chain headquartered in Grand Rapids,

Michigan hired her, and it was said she became the top women's wear buyer in the entire country. She had a big ego, and liked to mention that she was earning equal to what a man in the same position would make.

Ruth would frequently send us clothes as gifts, and always made it clear that they were expensive. None of these additions to our wardrobes was ever needed, but Mom would always write her a polite thank you note, and once again tell her that we had more clothes than our closets could deal with.

I spent a year in New York and she was there twice for fashion shows. She called and invited me, and I was pleased to go, just to meet the models.

Ruth had men friends, but she never married, as her job was her life. She enjoyed men fussing over her, something I never did. She even asked me to just call her Ruth in front of others, not AUNT Ruth. I played her game to a point, but there was a wall between us. I'm sure she felt it as well. The fact is that I went to college and she may not even have graduated high school, but was making a large sum of money. That was her distinction.

Despite the accommodations I'd make to please her, we never got along. She wanted to be the boss. For example, during that year in New York that I was acting, Ruth wanted me to leave the stage; she would get me a job as a women's clothing salesman! That was not for me and I politely refused. But to say no to Aunt Ruth was not a good thing. She didn't take it lightly when people refused to do her bidding.

When I left for Europe she didn't call, or write to wish me well. No surprise. I saw her only one more time. It was a few years after I'd moved to Europe, and I was back in the States for a visit. By this time, I had gone on not only to complete my studies, but also to establish myself financially in the European community. It was while attending a function at my brother's home that I again saw Aunt Ruth. I recall I wore a custom made Saville Row suit, intentionally, to impress her, and everyone else. If anything, I was probably a bit over the top and too cocksure of myself. Ruth and I barely spoke. She had aged and I was on top of my game.

Although she listed Steve as one of three people in her will, when Ruth passed away, she left him nothing. I was not mentioned at all. I never could figure out why she put him in there and then didn't give him a dime. Family or not, some people are just not meant to get along.

May she rest in peace.

Aunt Jeannie

Dad's other sister, Jeannie, was totally different. She married at about 23 and as I recall, it was to a nice fellow. I knew him as Sy. I've no memory now of his second name. I do remember that he was a CPA, and that they lived it a community called Levittown. We drove out there in our De Soto once, perhaps twice. Every house looked the same and there was no warmth. But it was new and modern and some people liked it. Different strokes for different folks.

They would visit us on occasion, but nothing stands out. Then the news came that they were moving to Korea, and later to Japan. Although young, I remember being fascinated by that. They had two young sons I have never met. Later I heard both of the sons became well regarded lawyers. When I asked how Sy could afford to send the two boys to Ivy League schools, I was told that the government takes care of that. I pushed for an answer and was finally told that Sy worked for a department called the Central

Intelligence Agency. When you work for the CIA, they take care of and basically run your life.

Both Sy and Aunt Jeannie passed away relatively young and within a very short period of each other. Before they left for Asia I saw them once for lunch. That was the last time we ever met. Almost strangers. I did make an overt attempt on one occasion to meet their sons but had no success. If they're alive, I have no idea. In any case, with their deaths, my family on Dad's side was slowly vanishing.

* * *

So, not a big family. However, I gave these family vignettes quite a bit of thought. I had a few other uncles, aunts and cousins. But what I've written about here are the people that I most recall. These are the ones who played a part in my early years.

CAROL

When it came time for my mother to go, she flew from Philadelphia to Los Angeles to be near my brother and me. The fact that I was living in Paris at the time was not a problem. Mom called me and said, "I'm flying to California in a few days. I would like you to be there. It's important." My mother never said that before. I immediately made preparations and flew back to L.A.

Meantime, almost as soon as Mom arrived in Los Angeles, she checked herself into a nursing home in Santa Monica. When I got into town and went to see her, she said, "This is it. I'm tired. I'm ready to go."

I was shattered. But I could see in her face, in her body, in her words what she was feeling, and I understood. She had gone down to 80 pounds, and it was clear the end was near. She didn't have the will anymore with the cancer to keep fighting and fighting. Enough was enough.

At that time, Carol and I had been meeting secretly, for about two years. We couldn't tell anyone because we were cousins. A few days after my first visit to see Mom in the nursing home, I asked Carol to join me. She did and we drove together.

We went into Mom's room. She was surprised to see us together and asked why we were. I explained that we were both going to come down so we thought we'd drive together. After just a few minutes of conversation, Mom looked at us and said, "That's not true. There's something going on between you two."

I explained that can't be because after all she's my cousin. My mother looked at us, smiled, and said, "There's no one else that's still alive that can tell you what I'm going to tell you. Your great-grandparents and Carol's lived a few doors away from each other in Russia and were close friends. They came to America almost at the same time, and the friendship remained between your grandparents and your fathers later. And now you and her brother Warren have been close friends all your lives. When you live so close to each other and know each other over a hundred years, you become like cousins. But there isn't a drop of blood between you from our families. We were just great friends."

Carol and I were stunned, and then explained to Mom what had been taking place. She passed away at 5:25 the next morning. It was almost like she stayed alive to pass this news on to us. If she hadn't, I don't know if we'd be together today.

I told this story at the burial and there wasn't a dry eye at the gravesite.

* * *

A few months after Mom died, Carol and I were at Charles de Gaulle airport outside Paris. She said to me, "We've been together for some time now. How come we're not married?"

Jokingly, I answered, "Well, you never asked me."

With that, Carol got down on one knee, clasped her hands together, and proposed.

I froze, embarrassed, and thought, "Oh, my God." But I couldn't keep the smile from spreading across my face. Reaching out my hand to help Carol up, I gave her a hug and said, "Yes." Other passengers around us broke into applause. We bowed, thanking the crowd, hired a car and drove into the City of Light.

* * *

PROLOGUE #2 TO A MARRIAGE

This story happened about two years before Carol and I spoke to my mother in her hospital room. I was living in both Portugal and Paris. Both marvelous cities to walk in. While I was in one of them someone called me on business and informed me I needed to fly to New York. So I got onto a plane, and attended another useless meeting.

Since I was in America, I decided to visit my younger brother and his delightful son and daughter in Los Angeles. They wanted me to stay with them, but I insisted on reserving a room at a nearby hotel. I'm rather used to doing this, as I sleep very little, just three to five hours a night, and enjoy a good drink while reading a book or even watching TV. My brother's family, on the other hand, are early to bed and early to rise, and I did not wish to interfere with their schedules. They were always aware of what they thought to be my rather bizarre lifestyle and they did not protest.

As luck would have it, my brother Steve saw our "cousin" Carol the next day and happened to mention I was on my way for a visit. She had got married years before, and had had twins. I knew her ex-husband very well.

In any case, the phone in my hotel room rang, and I was extremely surprised when it turned out to be Carol. She said that she was going out with a girlfriend for a drink and asked if I would care to join them. They collected me and we went to a nice place in Calabasas, quiet and relaxed. That's when Carol whispered that her friend was available and she thought I would like her. Then a very odd thing happened. Carol and I spoke further, about myriad matters, and I found myself getting very interested in HER! Her friend was somewhat bored and started having conversations with others around her.

After a few hours we decided to call it a night. Nothing had to be said. Carol and I took her friend home first, then went to my hotel. She came in for one more for the road and a bit more chat. I'll leave that evening there if you don't mind. Except to say that we proceeded to see each other clandestinely the rest of my week's stay. On the flight back to Portugal, I realized I had truly enjoyed this lady. But also came to the conclusion that as she was my cousin, there was nothing that could ever come from it. It was too bad, but I certainly did not want to start something that neither of us could finish...

But of course we couldn't leave it alone, either. After returning to Europe I called Carol and invited her to come to over to visit me. I wined and dined her, took her to Monaco, Cannes and Paris. And we obviously hit it off, though for two years we carried on a charade, with me referring to her as Monica whenever my family asked about whether I had a girl friend. My brother in particular would have had a heart attack.

ON THE VALUE OF ADVICE FROM WELL MEANING FRIENDS

It was in early March of 1997 that I was with my good friend Ian, walking down the Rue St-Germain in Paris. I was still spending a major part of my life there and in other parts of Europe. We sat down at a café, ordered some wine and proceeded not to speak for at least 10 minutes. Finally he looked at me almost in horror!

"Getting married is one thing," Ian said, "but she has TWO teenage daughters! And TWINS, yet! You're mad!"

I replied, "It would be an adventure."

"An ADVENTURE? If that's what you want, buy a motorcycle!"

I obviously did not heed his words and September 7, of 1997 I married Carol at the romantic restaurant Il Cielo in Beverly Hills, with her two young, bright and beautiful girls standing with us under the chupah. They were just preparing to go to college, Carrie to the University of Las Vegas and Cindy to The Fashion Institute.

Those years brought more adventures than FIVE motorcycles could have! I still recall the pride we all had at their graduations. They then entered their respective avenues of industry. Trials and tribulations followed, but they always moved forward.

Carol and I met some of their dates and I'm totally serious when I say NONE of them measured up to the standards we had set for both girls. Then Cindy introduced us to Andy and we felt immediately that he was the one for her. We've had the good fortune of becoming ever so close with Andy's parents, Niki and Taki.

The bigger shock came, however, when Carrie brought Gregg over. You see, Carrie always said that Jewish boys were nerds and that she would NEVER marry one. Carol and I could only smile. Here was a terrific, quality guy! We were not surprised when they made their announcement. Rather, we were thrilled! Then we met the rest of the mishpuka, Dee and Sy, for dinner. Lovely, and again, quality people.

My friend in Paris was mistaken. This has been a great adventure, and continues onward. I'm so very pleased I did not buy that motorcycle!

1940'S-1950'S ... GROWING UP

1957 Cuba

At the time of this photo, taken at a nightclub in Cuba, Alon was with Fabio (left), who was the brother of Alon's girlfriend Rachel, and Richard Ravitch (far right). Fabio and Rachel's father was the Vice President of Cuba. Shortly after this photo was taken, the family was "disappeared" by Castro, and the author never saw Rachel or Fabio again. Richard was the son of Duffy Shoyer, who owned the Kon Tiki clubs which dotted the Philadelphia area.

The PEPPERMINT STIK

2021 SANSOM STREET LO 7-8222

SANDWICHES

Strutburger ... 50
Flyburger (Melted Cheese) ... 60
Continental Steak ... 65
Continental Walk Cheese Steak ... 75
Pony (Ham) ... 60
Pony Special (with Cheese) ... 70
Slide Special (Grilled Cheese and Bacon) 55
Grilled Stomp (Grilled Cheese) ... 45

* All Sandwiches Served with Potato Chips and Pickles *

PEPPERMINT TWIST

Sizzling Hot Dog, Wrapped in Melted Cheese and Twisted Bacon, Surrounded by Crisp Italian Roll

55c

FRENCH FRIES ... 25

PIZZAS

Plain ... 1.00
Anchovies ... 1.25
Mushrooms ... 1.25
Pepperoni ... 1.25

Assorted Cheeses with Crackers 40c

BEVERAGES

Coffee (hottle) ... 35
Tea (hottle) ... 30
Peppermint Tea (hottle) ... 40
Hot Chocolate (hottle) ... 35
Orange Chocolate (hottle) ... 40

ICED BEVERAGES

? ? BLUE PEPPERMINT ? ? ... 30
Coca-Cola ... 20
Root Beer ... 20
Orange ... 20
Orangeade ... 30
Lemonade ... 30
Limeade ... 30
Grapeade ... 30
Iced Chocolate ... 40
Iced Tea ... 25
Iced Coffee ... 25

Chilled Cider ... 35
Steamed Cider ... 45

SUNDAES

Shimmy (Fudge) ... 60
Mess Around (Fruit) ... 60
Watusi (Crushed Cherry) ... 60
Stroll (Butterscotch) ... 60
Mashed Potato (Marshmallow) ... 60
Hully Gully (Nuts) ... 65

PEPPERMINT SPECIAL

Banana, (3) Dips Ice Cream, Chocolate, Cherry, Nuts and Fruits

90c

ICE CREAM SODAS

Chubby Checker (Root Beer Float) ... 45
La Pachange (Cherry) ... 45
Roach (Chocolate) ... 45
Slop (Vanilla) ... 45

* All Served with Whipped Cream and Jimmies *

Double Dip Plate of SHEARER'S ICE CREAM *"For Sheer Goodness"* 30c

Early Entrepreneurship

Alon partners with friend in nightclub for teens, p. 41. Remember the "Hottle"? And $0.45 sandwiches?

MY BIRTHDAY PRESENT

I don't know exactly which day it was, but a man was nasty and threatening a woman physically. My father stepped in to stop it, and my life changed forever.

My brother and I heard of the story, told to us by our mother, and were awed by it. Mom clearly was proud of Dad as she described his decisive move to stop what could have been a thoroughly unpleasant situation.

A few days later Dad said that I was ready for training. With no idea what he was referring to, Steve and I climbed into Dad's De Soto. We were stunned when he stopped at the police station at 57th and Pine Street. You see, we lived at 55th and Delancey, just a few streets away.

I was 8 years old, Steve was 5. We followed Dad and he seemed to know exactly where to go. Police stations have a lot of concrete and steel and are not welcoming places. Two large black men (not then known as African Americans) approached us, and greeted Dad as men do with old friends.

"This is Alon, my oldest. I'm entrusting him to you." He smiled as he looked down at me and said, "These men are my friends. Listen and follow all they show and tell you."

I had looked around and noticed some unusual matters. I pulled Dad down so that I could whisper into his ear, "Everyone here is black. We're the only white people."

To my embarrassment, he repeated every word I said out loud. "They're people … just like us. The color of their skin is darker. So what?"

I had no answer. I believe it was that moment that brought us all together. At least that's what I want to believe.

In no time I was in shorts, T-shirt and had huge boxing gloves laced onto my hands. I determined immediately that I was not going to be anyone's foil. You see, every Friday night I watched boxing on our black and white television. I watched and learned. A jab. A hook. A right cross. An uppercut. Move, move, move! Don't stand on a spot more than a second or two. Defense was very important. I watched, listened, and learned, because now I was a member of PAL, the Police Athletic League. At first the only white kid, but after my father's introduction, I couldn't care less. In time I fought perhaps 100 fights, and gained weight, height and muscle.

For about two and a half years, until the time we moved, I was at the gym, boxing and learning lessons of life. A great experience. I continued to practice wherever we moved. Self-confidence at that age was a marvelous feeling. Kids can be cruel sometimes, especially with the new kid on the block. I never was really challenged until later, but that's another, rather odd story.

* * *

I was now 12 years old, just two weeks from my 13th birthday. My brother and I were in Camp Green Lane in the mountains for the summer. Dad was doing well and felt it would be a good experience for us. With mountains, fresh air, lots of activities, it was indeed a fine place to be.

One day, as I was walking alone down one of the many pathways, I heard shouting. I looked and listened. Two of the older boys, about 15, were holding a girl prisoner against a tree. Angrily shouting four letter words at her, they grabbed the girl by her hair and pushed her down. She was partly crying and partly screaming at them.

When I saw one of them kick her I moved quickly. I pushed them both, which only provoked them. I told them to pick on a guy, not a girl. Then I saw the way they moved, and knew I had a fight on my hands. The taller one started with a punch to my head, opening a small cut. All I could do was smile and throw a left hook. It hit him hard in the face and he went down.

The other boy I just smiled at. Not tall but large in size, he went for me and I stepped aside easily. Within a few minutes he was breathing heavily. I hit him and he went down. It was all over in only a few minutes.

The girl held onto me and could not stop thanking me. I led her away and we spoke. Her name was Marsha and she was 15, almost 16. I felt foolish, but was honest and told her I would not be 13 for two more weeks. She didn't mind and suddenly I understood, I had my first real girl friend. On August 5th, the night of my birthday, there was a film being shown for everyone in the Food Hall. Marsha sat with me and after about 15 minutes said we should go and be alone. Although surprised, I agreed and we went inside an empty cabin. We relaxed on a bed. She went into her purse and removed a condom. I don't think I had ever seen one, let alone had one on.

It was some time, months, before I was to learn that Marsha was rather free with her favors and that I was being taught by a young lady of great experience. After camp she turned 16 and was given a car by her folks. That meant she could collect me and we would go to her home when her parents were away. She had two girlfriends as well whom I was to be with. You can imagine the rest. An interesting start for a boy of 13.

* * *

A few years ago Carol, my wife, and I were having dinner at Wheeler's Fish House in London. A lady came up to us and asked if I was that person she once knew. I smiled and replied, "Yes, Marsha." It was then her husband came to us, wheelchair bound and forever paralyzed. We smiled at each other knowingly. Life leads us down many paths.

HOW I GOT MY NICKNAME, ROCKY, AND ALL THE OTHER A.K.A.'S

August 5th, 1939... Someone at Saint Luke's Hospital had made a mistake. Perhaps it was an accent or an accident, but "Alon" was registered in the paperwork for the about-to-be-born child, instead of "Alan," the name my parents had planned on giving me. Once I actually arrived, it was too late to change, I suppose. But I was to learn over the years it really did not matter.

My Hebrew name was Eliazer, which was OK. The one name I NEVER answered to was Al! That was lazy and showed no respect for me. However, all that was going to change over the next generation or so.

On September 23, 1952, Rocky Marciano knocked out the esteemed fighter and World Heavyweight Champion, Jersey Joe Walcott, in Madison Square Garden. The very next day, the biggest fellow and bully in our high school, Billy Walters, picked a fight with one of my closest friends, Stuart "Buzzy" O'Dell, whom he outweighed by perhaps 70 pounds. Billy was also 5 inches taller than Buzzy. My friend was brilliant and would become a top Washington lawyer. He was also a good pal. But he had never been in a street fight in his life.

I approached Big Billy and asked why he didn't pick on someone his own size. I was no bigger than my friend, but I was not afraid of Billy. As I suspected, the bully had not many fights, because his sheer size put potential opponents off, whereas I already had 5 years in PAL, the Police Athletic Boxing League. Two or three days a week I would go there and put the gloves on with other kids and instructors. That was the period during which I had competed over 100 times. One tough Irish kid and I were the only two Caucasians there. McCoy was a big bull of a youngster, my age, and we fought against each other often.

In time I learned that size was not as important as other intangibles. Which is why Billy Walters didn't bother me a bit. There was an alley across from the school that the school had no jurisdiction over. Even so we were warned that we would be suspended if a fight took place. I smiled and looked up at Billy. I knew my unconcerned attitude was starting to trouble him. Mind games....I started to learn them young.

At 3:30 p.m., we and a few dozen other kids were in the alley across from the school. Before I was prepared, one of Billy's friends had yanked my jacket down in back of me, so that I could not lift or use my hands at all. But one of my friends jumped in and pulled the jacket off altogether. Now I was free to move and I was angry at that cheap trick. Big Billy attacked and I was ready for him. I sidestepped his charges and hit him two or three times in the nose. He leaped at me and my fist caught him in the eye. About that time I recognized that he had probably never been hit by anyone before, and that he was in a state of almost shock, seeing blood coming from his nose and under his right eye. I moved quickly, throwing a left hook and a right uppercut. Down went Big Billy. Mouths were open, speechless at the sight. Then someone in the crowd said, "Another Rocky Marciano." Then another said, "No, he's Rocky Mintziano." And for some years I was always referred to simply as "Rocky." This was long before the film had ever been dreamed of by Sylvester Stallone!

The moniker would turn out to be both an obstacle and a help. I had been turned into sort of a gunfighter, with fists instead of pistols. No one wanted to have to fight Big Billy; they would rather take me on. Beating me would be more of a big deal. I realized this and headed right for the gym. I explained to the trainers, all ex-fighters, what had happened and what could be lying in wait for me. They trained me much more seriously than they had been, and pushed my body almost to a breaking point. I had been correct. The street fights came, one after another. At least a few a week, until the kids understood I was not backing down to anyone.

The word had gotten back to my mother and father and the rest of the family. First shock, then some pride took hold. They began to see me as a young Jewish man who would never start trouble, but would not run away from it either. Now Mom and Dad started calling me Rocky all the time, as would their friends.

Some teachers were not fond of the appellation and my folks were asked to come to school. As always, they were dignified and polite. They calmly listened to the caustic remarks by my counselor, the principal and a few teachers. My dad stood and said, "Rocky is his name. That's how we and all his family and friends refer to him. If required, we will go to City Hall and legally change his name to Rocky. We would be grateful if you also called him by that name." Case closed. To this day, family and friends always use the name "Rocky." (Except in Europe where it's Alon.)

A few years later, I was sixteen, and we had to move to Florida, as doctors had advised Dad that he might never last through another cold Philadelphia winter. The heat and humidity were the best thing for his health. There were no second thoughts. Things needed to be dealt with quickly and we had to move to Florida, and so we did.

I was in my last year of High School and my head football coach handed me a sealed letter to give to the new football coach whom I was yet to meet. As much as we wanted to read it, it was never opened. I enrolled at Miami Beach High, then saw a soda pop shop where it seemed there were a lot of kids my age. I bought a soda and had a few light conversations with the kids there. Suddenly, a boy shouted, "It's those guys from Miami!" and everyone raced for the door. When I asked the guy behind the counter what the story was, he said they came around every so often to beat these kids up. He suggested I move on as well. I recall asking if they had two arms and two legs. Once that was confirmed I just sat in my comfortable chair. Seven or eight scruffy looking boys about my age walked in. As I was the only customer in the place they came and asked my name. "Rocky," I replied. "Rocky? Are you a fighter?" I smiled and said that I would be happy to take them on, of course one at a time. Like Big Billy, they were tough in a crowd. Not too anxious to try out the new guy who was not backing down, though, in a one on one. They made some remarks, but not one made a move. They left. No trouble. It wasn't ten minutes before the first group returned. The counter fellow told the story to them and even embellished it a bit. It seems like there was a new sheriff in town.

That whole episode may have helped me with the kids, but not with the coach. The next day I went to his office to say hello and give him the letter I had. He gave me a hard stare, read the letter and said he had already heard about me. It seems the little incident in the candy store had made the local paper, but now I was called, "Hard Nosed Rocky Mintz" from Philly. "I don't like trouble makers," he said. "Your old coach gives you quite a good review, and mentions you don't back down. But if you start any nonsense here, you're history … understand?"

He handed the letter to another coach who looked very pleased with it. His name was Gatton Vacarro, from Cuba. He and I became good friends. It seems he also did not care for people who backed down!

That was a very interesting period, but I did well and was noticed by colleges and universities. I took a dual scholarship at the University of Miami — for football and boxing — because I wanted to be near my dad, just in case he needed me. And frankly, when I visited there, I saw lots of pretty girls. That's when my name changed again and again and again.

One girl I was chatting up said she was on her way to a reading at the school theater and invited me along. The reading was for a play she wanted to be in. I sat there and listened to all the boys and girls read and thought to myself, "No one is reading the lines the way the author has written them." They were all reading the same two pages and I wondered why they hadn't memorized them by now. It was Thornton Wilder's play, "Visit To A Small Planet."

"NEXT!" They were looking at me! I was about to say I wasn't an actor, when the director said the magic words, "Are you afraid?" I remember looking at him and thinking, "I'll show you!" When handed the two pages I waved them off and approached the leading lady. (She was about 18 and NO, I was NOT afraid). I did what not one of the other fellows did and took her in my arms. Then, I calmly spoke the words from the script. Except I had most of it already memorized. When I finished, I boldly added a few lines to sort of close it out. The director then said, "OK, readings are completed, and YOU," pointing at me, "Come here. NAME?" I've no idea why now, but at that moment I could not use Rocky. "Alon," I said. "Alon Mintz."

"If you want to get anywhere in this business the Mintz bit will have to go!"

Thinking of my brother, I said, "How about Alon Stevens?"

The director thought about it for a brief moment and said, "Yes, that might work. We should spend the afternoon together and go over the entire script."

"No," I replied, "I can't do that today."

A peculiar look crossed the director's face.

Then I explained, "I'm not yet registered to attend the school. Don't you think I should do that first?"

His eyes bulged, his cheeks became red, and I thought he was about to pass out. "YES, yes, by all means DO register. That is quite important. How about tomorrow, Mr. ....Stephens?"

As football practice had not started, I agreed. The play was a hit and I enjoyed being on stage.

* * *

It was a few years later that I signed with the William Morris Talent Agency in New York. They changed the name to ADAM STEPHENS. Later, I signed with another agent who changed it to ADAM SAVAGE. I didn't want to ask Mom for money, and was quite fortunate in that I did a number of TV shows, and even some modeling.

A bit later I came to Los Angeles, and met a number of out-of-work actors. This was not a happy sight, and then my connection at the agency, which had been so promising, became problematic. I had an unpleasant encounter with my agent, Maynard Morris, one of the heads of the firm, which would have meant reclining on a rather odd casting couch. Clearly, "The biz" was not for me. More about this blip in my life in the story about Maynard Morris, page 49.

In retrospect, the encounter with Maynard worked in my favor. When I sat in the train back to Philadelphia from New York, I felt relieved. The experience actually was cathartic. And while I had enjoyed acting, I never looked back and regretted my decision to move on.

Shortly after my acting denouement, I decided to go to Europe to study medicine. My name once again became Alon Mintz, and remained so. Until I had to go to a number of Arab countries. Living in London at that time, I went to the British Home Office, as the travel was for the sale outside of Great Britain of British-made medical equipment, assisting growth of the country's exports. I met a delightful lady at the Home Office, who understood perfectly. She arranged for me to receive a new passport, only to be used when entering Muslim countries. That name? Ali Mintez.

That period of my life is over, I am pleased to say. I am once again, and will, I HOPE … always remain … Alon Mintz.

THE YEAR OF THREE ARRESTS

When I was sixteen and still living in Philadelphia, before we moved to Florida for my dad's health, I had a car, like some of my friends. We used to go to Marty and Bunny's Soda Shop. One time just as I got there my father pulled up, very upset.

"Some guys just beat up your brother!"

The boys he was talking about had come over from the Main Line, and wanted to beat up some Jews, frankly. I immediately rounded up all my friends and we drove out toward their turf looking for them.

One of the friends with me was Kenny Sylk. His father was one of the owners of Sun Ray Drug Stores. Today I understand he's doing fantastically well in real estate, and is a builder here, and in Israel.

Anyway, while we were driving I recognized two of the characters my father had described boarding a bus. Kenny took over the wheel of the car. I jumped out and ran onto the bus and attacked the two of them. One I hit, and heard his nose go. He just crumpled. The other one tried to fight back, but all I could think of was my brother and I kept throwing punches. I didn't realize that one of my punches had broken the second boy's jaw. What it looked like was that he was smiling at me.

The bus driver started screaming, drove the bus off the road, and kept honking his horn furiously. Finally the police came. I grabbed the two fellows and literally threw them out the front door. The police had their guns on me and I told them what they did to my brother, and who my father was. The police arrested all three of us. We spent that night in jail. For some reason they released one of the boys in the morning, and kept the one who was apparently the ring leader. And they kept me. The only laugh I got out of all this was that they made me take my belt off. Like I was really going to hang myself!

The police called the other boy's parents and mine the night we were arrested and told them they could come in the next morning. The first thing the boy's parents said was, "Are you in trouble again?" Then they said to my father, "He's nothing but trouble. We're not going to press charges." My father told them, "He beat up my son!" They didn't seem to care. The police let both of us go. I walked out of a police station, my first time ever having been arrested, a free young man.

* * *

Within the next six months I got arrested a second time. Again I was at Marty and Bunny's, this time looking for a parking space, when I saw the blue lights flashing in my rear view mirror. I stopped. The cop came over and said, "You're double parked. I'm giving you a ticket."

"But I haven't parked yet, Officer," I told him.

"Are you back talking me?"

"No, I just wanted to tell you I haven't parked yet."

And that's when he said, "You Jews have to learn." With that he hit me with his billy club. Luckily, I ducked my head and he got me on the side of my neck. Instinctively, I reached up and hit him on the chin. He went down. Next thing I knew, he had his pistol out, pointed at me. My girlfriend Mimi ran out and got in between us, and a bunch of my friends joined her. I assumed the policeman knew he would be in trouble if he fired. So he just said, "You're under arrest."

He put my hands behind my back, handcuffed me, and threw me in the back of his car. We drove only a little distance toward the station when he stopped the car, took the cuffs off and said, "Get out."

"No!"

"What do you mean, 'No?'" he yelled at me.

"You're mad and you're going to act as if I'm trying to escape. I don't want you to treat me as if I'm trying to get away."

He still had his pistol pointed at me. We were suddenly surrounded by my friends' cars — about seven or eight, all watching him. He put his gun back in the holster, and we went to the station.

Once again I was placed in a cell and my parents were called and told I would have to stay overnight. But I was extremely lucky. The son of a magistrate, Benjamin Seagal, had been there and witnessed the entire episode. He immediately told his father. The father was not due to be on the bench the next day, but because of my case, somehow had himself called to serve. They brought me to court in handcuffs. The policeman came in with his eye, mouth and nose bandaged, and his arm in a partial sling. My friends were stunned; they knew that this man was faking all this. The policeman told the magistrate that he'd been attacked by a group of young men. Seagal knew the truth and called someone in to look at the policeman's arm and to take off his bandages. There was nothing wrong. They were all bogus. Seagal said, "This case is dismissed immediately, but you," to the policeman, "are under suspension as of now." The man was later reassigned to a bad area in South Philadelphia.

* * *

The third arrest came about on Halloween evening that same year. My girlfriend Mimi, who looked like Sandra Dee by the way, and I — dressed as Doctor Malone and his nurse — had gone to a very large party; about 100 people were there. About an hour into the party, I was looking for Mimi and asking friends if they'd seen her. One girl asked, "Is she dressed all in white like a nurse?"

I said, "Yes."

"Well she may be in trouble. The last time I saw her some guy had her in the cloak room and they were fighting."

I raced back, didn't see them, and then I heard a muffled sound. When I looked over the counter I saw Mimi was on the floor, with part of her uniform torn off, and this guy was on top of her, trying to rape her. I recognized him, Dick Ronas — one of the wealthiest young men in town. I ran to them. I don't recall if he took a swing at me or not, but my punch connected with his nose, breaking it. There was a great deal of blood, making our costumes more appropriate. Mimi and I decided to leave.

A few days later I was served with papers to appear in court. I had an attorney, as did Dick. The judge called both lawyers up to the bench.

My lawyer told the judge, "It wasn't assault and battery, it was self-protection, and Mr. Ronas was trying to rape my client's girlfriend. We have no problem, nor does she if you wish to call her up. She'll give you a full statement."

It was as though an anvil dropped. Ronas' lawyer went into a discussion with the parents and Dick. "Your Honor, what sort of verdict will you be thinking of?" asked the lawyer.

The judge volunteered, "At this point I do see assault and battery, for self-protection, for Mr. Mintz. And I also see attempted rape for Mr. Ronas. Shall we proceed with the case?"

The other side declined quickly, and all charges were dismissed.

The funny thing is that Dick's father was one of the top ear, nose and throat physicians in the city. The boy tried to follow in his dad's footsteps, but failed his medical exams. He turned out to be one of the biggest drug dealers in Philadelphia.

* * *

I'm very pleased to report that later that year my attorney had all three cases involving me expunged from the record.

WILLY PASTRANO
5TH STREET GYM, MIAMI BEACH

YES, I had certainly heard the name Jake La Motta, The former Welterweight, Middleweight and even Light Heavyweight Boxing Champion of the World. He was a large, bulky man in muscle, and an unpleasant person. He had recently been in prison, where he spent a few years for taking advantage of a young girl. She made money on her back for him, and now you get the picture. Then he was released.

This story happened at the 5th Street Gym in Miami Beach. I was only 17, but already sparring in the ring with professionals. I sensed I was good, but had a lot to learn. I was determined to improve myself. I understood it would not be easy. I pushed myself to work harder than everyone around me.
In the gym, I had just knocked a boxer down, Irish Frankie Crawford. He was bigger and older and undefeated, but I suppose I was lucky. I caught him on the chin and he just crumpled. I'm still not sure which of us was more surprised. I helped him up. There was no animosity between us, just one good punch. He left the ring and I was still somewhat awed by what had happened.

After he walked out of the ring an unpleasant voice growled out, "Good punch, kid. Let's you and me go a few rounds." I immediately recognized La Motta's raspy voice. I turned and said to him, "Jake, you're twice my age and you've been a World Champion. You must be kidding! I'm 17, you're in your thirties."

He replied with something to the effect that this was not a big deal, he only wanted the workout. With reluctance I agreed. It was when

Jake entered the ring that I understood how massive he had become. Apparently prison had done him no harm. Almost at the offset, he tried to tear my head off. Half his age and 50 pounds lighter, my only chance was to move around him, at the same time throwing fast punches when I could slip them in. I suppose it was luck more than talent that allowed me to catch him with a very nasty punch on his nose. He became furious and attacked me. The men around the ring screamed at him to slow down. However, he heard nothing.

Suddenly another man appeared in the ring. He said something in Italian that La Motta heard, but couldn't care less about. He was a handsome guy, about five years older than I was. Big Jake smiled and suggested that he take my place. I wasn't pleased with that, but the guy gave me a wink or a smile and I understood and left, and he entered. Funny thing was I thought I stood a better chance against Jake than this good looking Italian did. But being the young person there, I shrugged and exited the ring.

The bell rang and La Motta tore after this new opponent. But the new guy wasn't there. He moved, dodged, and threw punches. All of which landed on Jake, who was being taken apart. Everyone was dumbstruck. A few minutes later Jake quit, saying fighting two fighters took a bit out of him. I was flattered. I was now a man, and a fighter! My hero? His name is Willy Pastrano. He went on to become the Light Heavyweight Champion of the World. I got to know him, and we double dated. He was just a wonderful person.

It was no surprise when I read that he was recently a hero in the New Orleans flood. But Willy liked food and girls a little too much, Although he went on to become the World Champion, he lost the title, and his desire to continue boxing within a few short years. But for a little while he had it all. I was pleased to call him my friend.

IRISH FRANKIE CRAWFORD

Irish Frankie Crawford, the guy I was fighting before Jake La Motta that day at the Fifth Street Gym, appeared as I was back in the ring sparring with one of the fellas, trying to perfect my boxing skills. As I mentioned, he was undefeated. He was a very flashy guy, with two girls hanging on his arms.

Once again I heard from a real pro words that somewhat alarmed but at the same time excited me, "Hey, kid, how about sparring with me?"

"Sure!" I said. Frankie was an excellent boxer, but he punched like a girl. He kind of tapped you, but didn't hit you hard enough to cut or hurt you. There's a name for that They call it Pitti-pat. It's not at all like when somebody like Muhammad Ali hits you; THAT you really feel.

Much to my dismay I soon saw that Frankie wanted to show off for the gals. At first he picked me apart with his boxing skills, but as soon as I realized he didn't hit hard, I attacked and got lucky, throwing a punch that knocked the undefeated Irish Frankie down.

It happened that a major trainer, Angelo Dundee, who later worked with Muhammad Ali, was there with his brother, the famous promoter Chris Dundee. When I left the ring, Angelo said, "Hey, kid, you're OK. You want to be a boxer?"

I was so impressed that he would even speak to me, I said, "Sure!"

"OK," he said. "What's your name?"

I told him.

"Are you Jewish?"

"Yeah."

"Do you mind wearing the star of David on your shorts? That'll bring the people in."

"No, I am what I am."

I remember running home afterward. My mother was in the kitchen cooking. I said, "Mom, great news! I just knocked down a big time fighter and Angelo Dundee, the famous trainer, said he would take me on and I have great potential. Isn't that great?"

She never turned around. Just kept staring down at the pot, stirring her sauce. "You will pack your suitcase and move out. Because I didn't raise sons to become fighters." When I complained, she said, "Talk to your father." I did, and he said it was great, but I should go back to school first, and then we can talk about it. With neither my mom or my dad in my corner, I had to tell Angelo what had transpired. The nice thing is he and I stayed in touch for many years. When he came to London we even dined together.

I never fought for Angelo, but later, when I was having trouble in my business, finding it hard to pay my employees, I began fighting. This was at a place called Gym and Tonic. Sparring one day with a few guys, I was approached by a gentleman who said, "You're OK. Would you like to make some money?" And he put me into the ring, where eventually I ended up fighting professionally in a number of different countries. Always under a different name. Because if my mother ever heard that I was fighting professionally, with big, tough fighters, without the heavily padded training gloves we wore when I was fighting other kids at PAL, she would be upset. And I certainly couldn't have that. But I was earning a lot for back then, say $1000 a fight. I could pay my employees. Maybe with a cut over my eye, but I would just say I cut myself on a closet door.

I did pretty well, and even my parents came to be proud of my success again. But eventually business and health dealt a knockout punch to my boxing career.

THE PEPPERMINT STICK

I have an old pal named Mitchell Lieberman. I suppose my oldest. We met in a summer camp many years ago. I think I was 11. Mitch is about three years older. He's one of those people you like or dislike. No middle ground. I've never known a person with a more obscene vocabulary, but he happened also to be extremely bright. I knew his mother and father and they were totally different. Class in every way. His father Jack was the founder of Liebco Brushes, one of the major brush companies in the entire world. They produced millions of almost every type of brush imaginable and still do today. Mitch never wanted to be in his dad's business. He always said he wanted to make it in life himself. Thinking about it, I would say he was reasonably successful. However, it didn't hurt that when Jack passed away, he left his considerable funds, millions, to Mitch and his sister Cookie.

One night we were sitting around a girlfriend's house, discussing the enormously successful New York club, "The Peppermint Lounge," and got into a serious discussion regarding how we might also embark on such an undertaking. I knew of a building for rent and decided to see if we could afford it. Amazingly, it was our old high school advisor who owned it. As neither of us had been "good boys," we doubted our advisor would rent it to us. But when we met, he laughed and said we were two of the worst students he ever had to deal with. Bad boys who always gave him a laugh. Then he smiled and said, "How can I not say OK?"

We were thrilled and spent two months redoing what was really just a very large garage. Not even a window. We ourselves built a rear door with bricks, and painted and added a small kitchen. Pepsi Cola had put up a big luminous sign for free, as that was going to be our house drink. We couldn't afford to even think of a beer or wine license. Besides, this was going to be for a young crowd, not adults. Long before Western Medical in London, I had earned my stock broker's license and also had a vending machine company. Thinking back, I suppose I was working almost 18 hours a day. A long time ago.

But while we were having a great time planning and equipping our club, we ran into a major problem. His name was Frank Rizzo, the Chief of Police in Philadelphia, a very nasty man. When he heard we were opening a teen dance club in center city, he was furious, thinking it would create problems for his police force. He could not have been more mistaken. We spoke and told him that we were not permitting anything remotely illegal. Not even cigarettes. His said a loud NO and we were concerned. But my uncle was Jack Alexander, the head of all licenses in the city, and he backed us all the way. We opened in November of 1961. There were about 200 seats and tables with red and white tablecloths. The first night we were full, with lots of adults including my mother, as well as kids. Then came the surprise. Chief Rizzo walked in with his pistols criss-crossed over his hip, a style that gave him the nickname "The Cisco Kid." Behind him were at least seven or eight other policemen. He raised his voice and threatened to close us down quickly. The adults stood, surprising him, and spoke up for us. He was to prove to be a bad loser.

We had a great club. Some people will remember Frankie Avalon, Fabian, The Shirelles, Chubby Checker, Sal Mineo and a host of Philly icons, all of whom were paid the same: $6 for three shows. We charged a $5.00 admission. It was a money maker. Six nights a week we packed the people in. We could have stayed open later, but not wanting to upset Rizzo, closed at midnight. Besides, we were now paying over $100 a week in graft to the local police.

Most nights Mitch and I went to a late night club, the RDA, and lived the good life.

However, nothing that good lasts forever. About eight months later Chief Rizzo took our dance and entertainment licenses away. I went back to my uncle, who reinstated them. However, he suggested we have a talk with Rizzo or there were other ways he could make life unpleasant for us. It took a number of calls to get an appointment, but then to our surprise, he relented. I explained that yes we were young, but we would never allow drink or drugs in our place. We were trying to create a safe environment for young people and rarely even charged adults. He listened calmly and said nothing.

Rizzo was a large man and used that to his advantage. He finally spoke. "You went to your Jewish Uncle and got your licenses back. You went over my head." I immediately explained that we had called him frequently to try to meet with him first. Rizzo then said, "I hear you have a lot of Wop friends in South Philly, Mafia town." I said we try to make friends everywhere. I certainly knew no one in the Mafia and it was my understanding that although it was used as a slang word against Italians, Wop really meant, "Without passport." It applied to all races and religions, referring to all those who emigrated here. Most Americans came from somewhere.

Rizzo stared at me. "And where did your parents come from?"

I said my dad was born in Philly and my mom in Florida. I looked at Mitch and he said his parents were both from here. Rizzo's ashtray was now full as he smoked some foul smelling tobacco. Silence filled the room. Finally, he said, "You people actually believe you can beat me?" His words, "You people" got to me.

Rizzo then told us we could keep our new licenses; there were other ways he would teach us no one ever won against him. We asked if there was anything we could do to prove to him we were good citizens and were trying constantly to work with the Chief and the police. He stood, bulk overhanging his large belt, guns protruding from his hips. "Nice talking to you fellows, good for a laugh. Now it's my turn to teach you never to mess with me again." Rizzo turned his back, not wanting to shake our hands.

When we left his office, it must have been five minutes before Mitch said, "It's over, you know." I just shook my head. Yes I understood, but was determined to fight on. Wrong. That night when I drove in front of the Peppermint Stick, I saw the police car parked in front. No officers in it. I asked Mitch why it was there. All he said was, "This is the beginning." People came and saw the car, shrugged, and the night went as usual. The next night there were three police cars there. No officers anywhere. The third night, there were five police cars there, but only a few officers out front. Those police we were paying came in, apologized, and said the orders were from the very top brass. One told us, "You boys are done. Face it. Get out before it gets worse." For once they did not ask for any money. The next evening even more police cars parked in front, as if we were the police compound. Dozens of cars, probably many of the same ones as had parked in front the nights before.

Rizzo's campaign against us did the job. People coming to just sing and dance took one look at the police cars in front and just kept walking. The club was almost empty the entire night. Mitch and I just looked at each other. We called our landlord who said he expected something odd to take place and drove there to meet with us. We had done such a good job fixing the place he was impressed. He told us not to worry about the lease. If we would leave it intact, kitchen and all, he would have no problem renting it. The three of us smiled and shook hands. Then we laughed and bonded with our old high school adviser, all a bit older, a little wiser and doing our best to enjoy life to its fullest.

We were only bitter about Chief Frank Rizzo for a short time. This tough guy had a heart attack only a few months later. It was reported that he had lived a stressful life. Mitch and I could only smile and hope we added a little to the pressure.

A SLICE OF MY LIFE'S HISTORY MIAMI....1957

My best friend Gary Engel and I had made plans to go out, find some girls and party that evening. As I was getting dressed my father came in and said he and my mother were going to the hospital, as he was having some chest pains and wanted to play it safe. It had occurred before and was not unique. Probably just needed to get some medication. My dad and I were extremely close and I immediately said that I would cancel my plans and go with him. He just laughed and said this was nothing new, and I should go out and enjoy myself. Reluctantly, I concurred.

Gary collected me in his car about 8:00 p.m. and we went off to our usual haunts to try and get lucky. We spent hours with some new girl friends and just past 2:00 a.m. decided to call it an evening, driving down Lincoln Road to my house to drop me off first. Suddenly, seemingly out of nowhere, a long black sedan pulled alongside us, much too close. The windows were rolled up and quite dark. We tried to see who was in the car but it was impossible. It came closer and closer to us and when Gary slowed down it did, too. Now it was almost touching our car. When Gary speeded up it suddenly came alongside and forced him to either crash into it or go onto the pavement. We hit the curb hard and fortunately stopped, only inches from a telephone pole.

The car sped away and we just looked at each other almost in shock. Gary's hands were shaking so we sat back to catch our breath. A police car pulled up. They saw we had not been drinking and were not acting foolishly, and listened to our story of what had taken place. We had no license plate to provide them for the other car, and to try and locate a big black car at that time of the morning was next to impossible. We calmed down, the police drove off, and we proceeded onward. Gary dropped me off and went home. It was now almost 3:00 a.m. and I went to bed very quietly.

At 7:30 that morning I was gently shaken by a friend of my father's. I could hear other voices and knew something was very wrong. A few minutes later my mother's arms were around both my brother and me. We were informed that Dad had passed away that morning in the hospital. Later, Gary and his father came to comfort us and offer condolences. Then someone asked what time was it that Dad had passed on. When told, "A little after 2:00 a.m. this morning," Gary and I could only stare at each other.

Was the black sedan simply a coincidence or was it a notice of something tragic that had occurred? Gary and I never spoke of it, even to each other. To this day, it was something unexplainable and will always remain as such.

1960'S

Contact Sheet for Adam Savage
a.k.a. Alon Mintz

NEW YORK AND MAYNARD MORRIS

I did a number of plays at the University of Miami and frankly earned quite a bit of acclaim. After one particular performance I was approached by a man named Maynard, representing the William Morris Talent Agency at the time (he later set up his own shop). I was praised and told that if I ever was in New York, I should stop in and see him. I assured him I would.

After Dad passed away and we moved back to Philadelphia I came across Maynard's card. I discussed it with Mom and took a train to New York. After making an appointment with the man's personal assistant, I went into his office. He treated me like a long lost son. We left soon to go to an expensive show business restaurant. The maitre d' and waiters treated him like a god; I was made to feel like his boyfriend.

At a guess Maynard was in his 60's; I was in my early 20's. Over lunch he told me that there was so much that he could do for me. Films, TV and personal appearances. I would make a great deal of money. Then he leaned down and under the tablecloth, touched my knee. Of course I had heard rumors, but this was nothing I had ever experienced. I froze, then moved his hand. He smiled and said he was making a special dinner in his apartment in Soho that evening, and was certain I would enjoy the affair. I said I would attend.

When the time came, I knocked on his door and he opened it with a flourish, saying, "Dear boy, do come in!" *Said the spider to the fly,* I thought, particularly as he was wearing a red dressing robe. We moved further into his rather lavish flat, which was, I must admit, interesting. No one else was there yet, and it was quickly apparent that it would be just him and me. My nerves were in a twist. I knew I had to be cautious.

We went directly to his dining table. I don't recall what we ate. Nothing to remember. I do recall his constantly filling up my wine glass. However, even as a young person I loved wine and no doubt I was a very expensive date!

After dinner we sat on his oblong purple sofa. Maynard tried to impress me with all of his contacts. I showed little enthusiasm. He recognized this and brought over a book of the male actors he represented. Many were major names, in various stages of nudity. Maynard said he could find me a great deal of acting and modeling work, almost immediately. Oh, I felt feelings. None of them remotely clean. I clearly said that I had heard it all before and talk was cheap. I thought a female actress would have said the same thing.

He touched my knee and I stood up. Then we did a scene that Billy Wilder would have been proud of. I started walking around his sofa and he followed me like a dog in heat. The walk progressed into almost a canter and eventually his age stopped him. "OK!" he said. "In a few days my PA will call you and you will be working. NOW, dear boy, after I've proven myself, you know I will expect you to show your appreciation."

I shook his hand and repeated, "Talk is cheap, but thank you for dinner."

I had no idea what would follow. Then his PA called. Two modeling interviews and five serious potential acting jobs. I nailed every one of them. Then Maynard called to collect. He said, "There will also be a new TV series, "Billy The Kid," and you will be perfect as Billy."

Later Maynard's personal assistant called with an invitation to dinner at the man's house. Just the two of us. Of course he never knew that the PA and I had become very close. I'm certain she was not pleased when she had to announce, "This dinner will be put up or shut up."

I said to tell him I was ill with the flu. Another actor, Clu Gulager, got the part. I've no idea who his agent was, but it really didn't matter, as I had already taken the train back to Philadelphia.

POCO

Early in the summer of 1965 I found myself with free time available one day. Friends had suggested that I see Big Bear Mountain and Lake Arrowhead, which were only a few hours from Los Angeles, where I lived. Thus, this morning I had got into my car alone and driven to the area. To this very day, I have no idea why the following took place. I don't really care for driving and perhaps should have reconsidered the entire adventure.

* * *

After a few hours on the road, I found myself in the mountains, and, foolishly, lost. Rain appeared though it was predicted to have been a sunny day. I ducked into a little market for directions, and at the cash register met part of my next life — a girl in need of a very small amount of money — a quarter to be exact. Yes, 25 cents. But to the shopkeeper, paying even a quarter less than the price of the item anyone wanted to purchase was not acceptable. The young lady in front of me told the store owner that she lived nearby and would return with the correct change. But her claim fell on deaf ears.

She had an unusual but lovely look. For some inexplicable reason, I felt an attraction to her. I immediately put the correct amount of change on the counter. They both looked at me and accepted the coin. As I walked from the store, the girl followed me and asked, "Please wait here. I live with my parents just up the road and will get you your money back." It was just change. But she asked me to wait, said she would speak with her father and return with the quarter, as what she had bought was for him. The rain was falling harder and I offered, almost insisted that I drive her to her house. I said I was not some weirdo and I would give my license to her or the store manager if there was any concern. She then said, "I'm an American Indian. Part of the Chippewa Nation. My father used to be a chief, which is the name everyone calls him. My American name is Jane."

She was anything but a plain Jane. Tall, wonderful figure, obviously strong, stunning high cheekbones and a full head of dark hair that flowed over her shoulders and almost touched her waist. I've no idea why, but I said she did not at all look like a Jane to me. More like Pocahontas. In fact, I asked her, "Would you be offended if I called you Poco?" She surprised me with a happy and charming laugh, and said that she thought that was great and fun, but if I met her father or mother, I should call her Jane. Apparently their humor was limited. Of course I agreed.

"Just up the road" turned out to be actually over two miles and now the rain was truly coming down. She was not troubled by any of this, except that her parents would now see her with a young man! I assured her I was not overly concerned as I had met people from all walks of life. Her reply was, "I'll bet you never met anyone like The Chief!" She was so right.

He was a very large man in every way. A fat face, large stomach, massive hands and a long ponytail. He was dressed like an Indian from a different time. At first he only wanted to give me the change from the store. He hardly looked me in the eye. Poco had said something about his drinking and I asked if there was any place open that he and I could enjoy a beer or two. He perked up and said he could get us into a private club, but mostly Indian. I said I wasn't concerned about that, because I would be with a chief and I had just had a good week financially. He was now my best friend.

I drove and Chief directed me to a cabin-lodge I would have never found. I obviously was a bit concerned, but it was just another challenge. As I was buying, the man drank and drank ... but he also asked me questions. What did I do, where did I come from, my family, my thoughts of the future, was I really ok with Indians? Did I want children, did it matter if they were boys or girls? Real men want boys to turn into men. Then he let his guard down a bit and said that he really wanted a boy but had the bad luck to have a daughter. Furthermore, his almost useless wife could no longer have any children. Then he said his daughter was certainly a virgin and in times past, he could have been paid well to provide her to another Chief. I said I wasn't interested as we just met hours earlier. He only smiled and said one is the same as another. If they could deliver boys, that was their only real gift. Cooking, sex, they all could provide that.

Somehow, with the help of another Indian from the club leading us in his car, we found our way back to the family's cabin. Poco and her Mother took Chief and placed him onto his own private bed. I was very tired and the torrents of rain had not let up. I slept in the back room on a bunk bed with every insect in the world.

In the morning the Chief was gone and Poco and her mother were as nice as one could wish for. The rain had stopped and the sun was making a brave effort to reappear.

Before I left I gave Poco my telephone number and insisted she call me if she ever wished to visit Los Angeles. I drove home slowly, trying to take in all that had happened the previous day and evening.

A few days later the phone rang late at night. A very quiet, almost whispering voice said, *This is Jane, or Poco as you called me.* "Yes," I replied. "Of course. Are you all right?" *The Chief is angry. I have only a few minutes to speak. Were you really serious about having me stay with you in Los Angeles?* Her voice sounded frail. I replied, "Yes, I am." She asked if we could meet in San Bernardino the next afternoon and mentioned a particular parking lot. I said, "OK." We settled on 5:00 p.m., just before nightfall. The next morning I called a friend, "Big Dave." He agreed to join me, as I just wasn't certain if I was being lured into something unpleasant.

We parked where Poco had told us. Minutes later a small pickup truck pulled alongside with just her and the Chief. He was surprised to see Big Dave, but said nothing about him. He looked me in the eyes and said, "So you will look after Jane now?" I only nodded yes. He handed me an envelope and made a comment that I would need to feed her. But if she were a boy, he would not be meeting with me. I noticed what appeared to be blood on a napkin. Later I discovered Chief had driven a fork about an inch under her right eye to make certain Poco understood his words. He took her arm roughly, and said, "Remember what I told you. Listen and obey this man."

I should mention I was only three years older than she was. There was no kiss or hug or any affection, he just went to his truck and drove off. Dave and I were both stunned. I opened the envelope. It had twenty dollars in it. His value of his daughter.

We dropped Dave off at his place and I drove us to my home, which now had another resident. I gave her a tour, and she was amazed that she actually had a choice of two bedrooms, neither being with me. She only had a small suitcase with very little inside it. I ordered a pizza and opened a bottle of wine and we talked for some hours. Finally I said we could both use some sleep. I may have kissed her cheek or forehead, I don't recall.

I went to my bedroom rather exhausted. About an hour later Poco opened my door and gently lay on the bed next to me. I asked," Is this what The Chief ordered you to do?" She nodded yes. "Are you really a virgin?" She was almost shaking but again nodded, then spoke. "Yes." I then told her to try and forget everything the Chief had told her. Those days were over. We smiled and had a hug, that's all. And then went to sleep.

Poco stayed with me about a month and although we enjoyed each other's company, we both understood that it was time to move on. She and I had been to a party and the two girls who lived there invited her to move in. It would help them with the rent. She did and we all remained good friends. She went to night school, worked days and sent her mother money without the Chief knowing.

Life isn't perfect. She was on a date with the other girls and a guy somehow spiked her drink. She was raped and when the call from the other girls came, I practically flew there. The guy was caught and received a long prison sentence. But Poco was pregnant.

The Chief never believed that a female could be raped. Had she called her parents she would have either been turned away or the Chief could have done something far more fatalistic. I dare not guess.

I cannot tell you how I thought it up. But she signed an annulment paper saying we were never married. We never were. I then arranged a wedding and party at a restaurant on La Cienega Boulevard. Many friends we knew attended, including my mother. The ceremony, the paper, even the priest were fictitious. Poco's mother and the Chief knew none of this and were thrilled. He actually gave me another envelope. This one had fifty dollars in it. She whispered to them that she was pregnant and was certain it would be a boy. The Chief was totally thrilled and was making all sorts of plans for his grandson. He would even build a separate bedroom so that the youngster could live there for months at a time. He would teach him how to be a man!

The baby of course was a beautiful girl. Chief never knew that. All he was told was that I was killed in an accident in Europe and that Poco was taking our son there to oversee the situation. A large financial estate was left to her and she would be in contact with them when time permitted. We last saw each other at Point Dume near San Diego about 1969. She had been accepted at the University there on a partial scholarship, in medicine.

To my knowledge, she lived happily ever after. Sadly, with my move to Europe and hers to San Diego, we lost touch so I don't know for sure.

STAR-CROSSED

Somewhere in 1965 I was packing for a flight out of Los Angeles, to get to Las Vegas. The journey, which I had to postpone, turned into a life changer, though I didn’t know it at the time.

It began as friends were about to drive me to the airport. When one of them offered to take my luggage and load it into the car, I protested, insisting on picking up the bags myself. But as soon I lifted the heavy suitcases, I was wracked with pain. Excruciating.

I dragged myself to my regular GP, who recommended two or three specialists. The man I chose decided that I needed surgery, a double laminectomy, to fix the problem. This is a procedure that removes a portion of the vertebrae that have become damaged and cause pain.

I was admitted to Cedars of Lebanon (now called Cedars Sinai Hospital), where I was delighted to learn that the room I was assigned to fell between those of Peter Sellers and Jeff Chandler. It seemed we all had lower back injuries. Operations were required for the three of us. Mai, Sellers' girlfriend, often asked me to turn the music up or down on my victrola, as it was either too loud or too soft.

Once the medical team finished sticking needles into my spine over the course of three weeks, I was told that the procedure was successful. However, the doctors also said that I could expect back and leg problems for the rest of my life.

There was no way I was prepared to accept that verdict. I was not ready to sit behind a desk for the rest of my life. I read about treatments all over the world. Then I read that I could continue taking medical courses in Brussels), at a university where they placed an emphasis on back problems. While I was in Brussels, at the university, I decided to try to build up my legs (which had indeed been affected by my back) by returning to boxing. The administrators at the university found out, and thought so highly of my persistence, that they decided to bestow upon me a full body (scholarship. While I attended the school, I also took courses on mind control. That year was marvelous and altered my entire future.

BRUSSELS, BELGIUM ... 1965

I took a year off from life, still mourning over my father's passing away. With my back injury on top of this loss, I was not at all certain what I wanted to do later in my life. I was just a young man trying to put the pieces in place. But I did know that I wanted to pursue studies at the university that offered those courses in treating back pain. Thanks to the European edition of the Paris *Herald Tribune*, I saw an ad that quoted a very low price in a boarding house in Brussels, in the center of town, near the university. Better still, it was also a short walk to the Grand Place, which offered lots of restaurants that served mussels and French fries, and a beer at less than a dollar. It was almost perfect. Just almost, as I was on the top floor. The 7th. No elevator of course.

Visualize a huge square, and place four cubicles inside it, one in the North, one South, the others East and West. With a heavy dark cloth curtain serving as a door your only privacy. There were three other young men about my age sharing that floor with me, in the other cubicles. We each had the same "luxurious" accommodations. Each cubicle had a single bed, a small closet, a bureau and a desk. In the center of the room was an old, stark, battered wood table that we could dine on, with plastic plates and old metal utensils on a shelf just above it. Stark, yes. But it was clean and for us it was all we required. The good news was the ceiling was glass and in the mornings the light from the sky poured in. Of course, the rain also seeped through.

When Mrs. Marceau, the owner, saw that I came down those seven flights every morning to shower in the only shower that existed in the building, that one being in the basement, she was upset. First she wanted to know if I had some skin disease. The average tenant showered once, or at most twice a week. Why else besides some skin problem would I shower every day? It was unhealthy and bad for the skin, she said. I assured her I did not have a disease, that I just enjoyed being clean. She then said she would have to charge me more, to cover the cost of the water. I smiled and said I understood. She never went forward with her threat.

In one of the cubicles in Mrs. Marceau's 7th floor flat there was Vincenzo. Last name I've long forgotten. A young Italian, who reminded us every day that he was a Communist. However, one night when I asked him to spell the word Communist, he couldn't. He had to buy the wine for us that time. In fairness, he was very passionate in his belief, even if he had no idea what he was talking about.

Across from his curtain was Vacent Patel, from Calcutta, India. He had been trained as a pilot by the Indian military. Something happened there he would never discuss, and he left and somehow ended up in Brussels, absent without leave. Quiet and meditative, he was the sort of person you could trust. He would laugh with us and was a true gentleman.

In the cubicle next to him was Tankama Odoon, a young black guy from the Belgian Congo. He had witnessed his family and others slaughtered by the rebels, called by the name Mau Mau. They were a large group — about 15,000 strong — who smoked gangi and drank to get very high, with blind faith in leaders who told them they could never die as long as they were with their army. I have no idea why the regular Belgian army did not try and stop them. Fear? The cost? Politics? I've no idea. Worse than cannibals, they rampaged and killed horribly the nuns, missionaries and anyone who would not join them. Months later a South African named Red O'Houre brought in a hired group of only 700 well trained mercenaries and decimated their numbers.

Before the Mau Mau's were defeated, Patel, Tankama and I signed on to go to the Congo. Vincenzo would have, but he said he was an Italian lover, not a fighter. Three times the other three of us were supposed to fly in and deliver supplies. Luckily for us, we never boarded any of the flights. Two of the three planes we almost embarked on never returned. The other was commandeered by the more experienced older men. We had studied and trained and were ready to do what was required. However, Red O'Houre and his merciless private army not only destroyed the Mau Mau's, they took no prisoners. It was slaughter after slaughter. In hindsight, we were pleased we were never called upon. We were still young and naïve, not prepared for that world.

* * *

Over the time we were together, we "roommates" heard each other's stories, cried and laughed at many. Young men, different in so many ways, but in a very short time we were like brothers. Our Belgian neighbors actually learned to like us. We fought, drank and got into all sorts of precarious circumstances. We learned from each other various matters that a tourist would not see or learn, with regard to the country each of us had left behind. As the months passed, we confided in each other as though we were a family. Some places refused entry to anyone that was not white. Well, that was two of us, but it was all four that took umbrage. We were a team, with no one left out. Of course there were love affairs and girls, some I could certainly write about, but this is perhaps not the best venue to do so. We shared joys and disappointments, successes and failures, some tears. But mostly we shared laughter. An odd point was that no one had a best friend. We seemed to care for each other equally.

Then a message came via the one telephone downstairs for Vincenzo. Good and bad news. His father was very ill and he should return if he wanted to see him before it was too late. Also, his application to the University of Rome was accepted. He was upset but excited. We stayed up all night, allowing him to talk all he wanted. His departure cut into us deeply. It also raised questions within each of us.

Vacent Patel greatly missed his family in India. His parents were not young and he had a number of brothers and sisters. I suggested that he go to the Indian Embassy in Brussels and see what penalty he would be charged with if he went back. It was hours until his return and I was extremely concerned that I had given him bad advice. It wasn't until dinner time that he came waltzing in, a delighted smile on his face. He learned that they could not and would not extradite him from Belgium. When he heard that, he knew he had room to negotiate. If he would rejoin the Indian Air Force, they would fly him back, and not penalize him for desertion. No back pay of course and he would be demoted one rank. They needed experienced pilots and were prepared to take him back. He was overjoyed!

We all put in funds to pay a lawyer so that Vacent would have the embassy's promise on paper, and duly signed; we were somewhat dubious of their verbal promises. Their ambassador did not back down, and signed the paper. As he boarded the bus to the airport Vacent promised to call and write us soon. When we heard nothing after a week we called the phone number he gave us, as his brothers. We were told that they knew nothing of Vacent's return, and that no one in the family had heard from him. To this day, as I write this, I have some guilt on my conscience for suggesting that he go and speak with his embassy.

Tankama and I now had the entire 7th floor. Two other young men came to live in our friends' rooms. They were a bit younger and cold. I had finished my semester at the University, read about this place called Israel and decided to go there. Tankama now had a girl friend that he was going to move in with. I still have a charcoal drawing that he gave me. Not great art, but the heart and soul that came with it will never allow me to part with it.

Every now and then my mind wanders to the three of them. Are they alive? Did they accomplish their dreams? I could have never planned for four totally different individuals to share one large floor in another country. It was an incredible experience. I don't believe we can plan these times; they just happen. And when they do, all we can do is smile and recall how fortunate we were to have been there.

BRUSSELS — A SPECIAL PERSON AND I

It was on Icelandic Airlines that I sat next to a charming girl named Margaret. We were like so many young people, backpacking and anxious to discover Europe. She was six foot tall in her bare feet, inches higher with shoes on. There were no designated seats so I just asked if she minded if I sat next to her. I wasn't trying to make a move, just have a nice conversation on a very long propeller-driven flight.

When the world ends it will look like Reykjavik, Iceland at 5:00 a.m. That's where we stopped to refuel. She asked me to call her Maggie as we were in the middle of such a long – 18 hour – flight, and I was pleased. We discovered we had things in common, and the rest of the trip became a delightful journey. When we landed outside Brussels, we took the train into town and rented rooms without seeing them or going through a travel agent. We had no idea what they looked like before moving into them, only that they were affordable. Not more than five dollars a day, and both on the same street; it was only a short walk from the University of Belgium, where we were both attending classes.

Maggie was so bright that I mostly said nothing and just listened to her. She occasionally spoke about times and places in history that I hardly knew of. She had an intelligence I greatly admired. Although she was somewhat embarrassed about her height, modeling had been good to her bank account. At the train station in Brussels, we shared a taxi that drove us first to her bed and breakfast. A problem occurred almost immediately. They hadn't known she was female and had her sharing a room with a couple of guys; she was adamant this was not acceptable. They refunded her money and we walked to my building. The women who ran the place was pleasant, and found a room for her on the fifth floor. It was not surprising that there was no elevator. Mine was on the roof, the seventh floor, sharing with three fellows I wrote about in the last story: one guy from the African Congo, one from India, one our resident Communist from Italy. We were all about the same age and somehow, we had taken a liking to each other.

My roommates saw me with Maggie as I was helping her find a room, and didn't give me much time before picking on me for being with someone of her height. Nonetheless, I went and persuaded her to join us for dinner. She did, and an evening filled with laughter ensued. Later, I walked her to her tiny chambers. Cheek kisses are just not the same. But she was good people.

The next day we all went to sign up for various classes at the University and helped each other work things out. Afterward we discovered our new home away from home, "The Grand Place," with the concrete statue of the little lad peeing away. As promised, there were lots of cafés serving mussels, fries and beer, all affordable if you watched your budget. Neither Maggie nor I were beer drinkers, but could accept the house wines. Rough as they were, with prices just over a dollar a bottle we were not about to complain. Later, when we became so-called regulars at one café, I noticed our wine had improved, thanks to the waiter. Students looked after students.

In addition to taking medical courses, I had a double major at the University, French and European Literature, and after a year received certificates in both. I also worked hours every day selling second-hand vending machines. Maggie took many courses and was getting funds from home. The three lads took all kinds of subjects, mostly where there were girls. Art of the human body was very popular. I admit, I likely would have enrolled in those

courses, but I felt it might lower me in Maggie's eyes, so I never did. All this time, there was still only the rare kiss on the cheeks for me. Bizarre! Everyone else assumed we were sleeping together ... I never even attempted it. Her respect is all I truly wanted. We could talk about so many things for hours.
I had a small but comfortable room in my shared apartment. There was a little desk for my old manual typewriter, and a single bed a bit more than I needed in size. But best of all, there was that skylight, from which I could see the sky day or night.

Occasionally, Maggie would wear three inch heels, and remember, she was six foot tall. There were some laughs at us. But she was just so bright. She was aware that I had a history with females. She knew I had had lovers previously. Nevertheless we grew to love each other, but did not in a physical way. She wore a silver Jesus cross around her neck that I noticed the first minute I met her on the plane. Then one day I saw it was no longer there. When I asked, she replied that she had been reading about the Holocaust and decided to put it away. She knew I was Jewish and wanted to make me more comfortable.

Then on a very nasty rainy night, Vincenzo, our resident Communist, opened the heavy maroon curtain "door," and there was Maggie with pizzas and wine. She had gotten a check that day and decided who better to share it with than us, her best pals. We stayed up late. Everyone tried to play and sing using Vincenzo's beautiful guitar, which really did not make him very happy at first. However, in time the food, especially the peppers and wine, did the trick. A fabulous evening with friends. Maggie did slip in the comment that she had to go back to the States, somewhere in the Midwest for a few weeks, but she was paying for the establishment to hold her room.

That night my three friends finally went to bed and I took her into my little cubicle to show her Tankama Odoon's drawing that he had gifted me with, an oil painting from the Belgian Congo. Not very good art, but it had a meaning that moved me greatly. Yes, I still have it more than 40 years later. We viewed it by candlelight, sitting on the bed. Maggie had tears in her eyes. She then completely shocked me. Holding it, she said, "We may never have another chance ... Please, I want to make love with you." I realized that this tall lovely girl had put off all her previous beaux. Why me? She didn't wish to discus it. "Let's not ruin a wonderful night with talk. Hopefully, there will be plenty of time when I'm back," she told me. I took her to the taxi in the morning and she was radiant, stunning. She left for the airport waving to me in the rear window. I was left wondering what she meant by "Hopefully."

In the three weeks that followed, I received only one short letter from Maggie. She asked about the guys and me, in the warmest ways. There was a special note to me that was odd, as if she had to watch what she was writing. I couldn't even call her as I had no phone number.

Later, a man called who identified himself as her father. I raced to the one pay phone we had in the house. "Is this Alon?" I heard. I identified myself. All he said was, "Margaret has gone to a better place. I promised her I would call to inform you. The cancer was overwhelming. You people made her last weeks pleasant, for which her mother and I thank you very much." I said that she made our lives happy, and was about to add happier than ever before, but was cut off by his, "Thank you." Then the line disconnected.

She was here for a short visit, but made an impact that her parents will never know. I told no one we had lost her. The memory of her will be precious always.

RICKY ... BELGIUM AND ISRAEL

I mention later in this book a baby born at the Police Hospital in Cairo, Egypt, delivered by my friend, Dr. Adel El Kady. The baby boy was given two names, Adel and Ali, the Ali being a tribute to me, the Adel to my friend the doctor who delivered him. It was rewarding and lovely to be so included in that baby's naming. I also mention that it was the second baby to have been given a name of mine. This is the story of the first.

Although I knew nothing of the University of Belgium in Brussels, if you recall, I had signed up for evening courses in medicine, French and European History there. I am rarely intimidated, but this university was comprised of a huge, dark stone group of buildings that one would hardly call a "campus," and just looking at the place, I got the feeling that studying would not be easy here. But being determined, a week later I attended my first class.

As I viewed the members of the class, my eyes met with those of a girl named Ricky. After the class was over, I had a pleasant surprise: she was just standing there in the hall. When I approached her, she didn't smile, but just said, "I know a family in Israel named Mintz. Are you Jewish?" I asked if it mattered and she quickly said, "Yes." I told her I was and she asked me to prove it. In jest I asked if she wanted to see my circumcision. "No," she said, with a smirk. "Just say something, anything in Hebrew." My vocabulary in that language was as poor as my knowledge of her country, but I tried. "Baruch Atah Adonai, Eloheinu Melech Ha-Olam, asher yatzar et ha-adam betzalmo, b'tzelem dmut tavnito, vehitkon lo mimenu binyan adei ad." She smiled for the first time. "Not bad. I believe you. Come, buy me a coffee and we can talk." It turned into quite a conversation.

She was attractive, although not a movie star. About 5'4", with a strong, sinewy figure. Eyes and vocabulary that expressed the fact that she was quite bright. We liked each other and became close. Not love. Just like-a-lot. We became a couple, which was OK. Not wonderful, just OK. We understood it would not be forever. A few months later she approached me with stunning news of the day. A rather small ship, the Belu, was sailing from Naples to Haifa. Very affordable, it carried cars in the bottom hold as well as passengers. I believe it was $295.00 for both my car and me. I never imagined I would be going to Israel, to the Middle East. It turned out to be a momentous voyage and one which changed my entire life.

For some reason the males had to share a cabin with other males, unless you could prove you were married. I shared a large cabin with three other guys. One of them was about five years older. His name was Israel Goren. We seemed to hit it off and spoke of a vast amount of issues. He eventually told me of his wife, Ora, who was attacked and left for dead. Even the Israeli doctors had given her little chance to survive. But he met a homeopathic doctor who said he might be able to save her. They took her down to the sea every day, kept her in the water for hours and made her exercise even when it was thought she was gone. They saved her life and she eventually became the country's Director of Tourism, and had three healthy sons. All became soldiers like their father.

I said my farewells to my shipmates as we came into port, then drove my Volkswagen off the dock. Ricky told me that I could leave her there and she would take various busses to her village where her family lived, a place called Kiriot Shimon, I believe. Being a gentleman, my thought was I would drive her to her family's house, call Israel Goren from there, and arrange a meeting with his doctor. I wanted to see if he had some possible help to offer me for my back.

Nothing took place as was programmed in my mind … And life changed. After arguing Ricky finally agreed that I could drive her to her relatives', and we went on to her village miles away. There was a small white house occupied by her sister, her sister's husband and their two children. I soon learned that my car was the only one in the entire area. Tanks, troops, and barbed wire were the realities that awaited me. Despite conditions, the family was very pleased to have Ricky back and made me feel very comfortable. Simon, husband of Ricky's sister, showed me where I should park my car, out of sight from the shooters hiding on the Golan Heights above. Although occupied by Israel since the previous war, the area still had spots where one or two terrorists could hide.

Ricky and I slept in sleeping bags in the living room, and in the morning she and her sister made coffee and tea, with a variety of fruits to enjoy. Not fancy or exciting, but certainly healthy. Later Simon and I went to check on the car. Shots rang out. Within minutes Israeli soldiers were with us to see if we were OK. After they brought us back into the house, much dialog in Hebrew ensued. I did not understand a word. I became tired of being crunching up inside the not very large house, carefully stood up, and went back out to my car. The bad guys had seen the vehicle — it really stood out in the neighborhood — and now it had holes in it that were not there when I'd bought it. Remember, this was 1965, a time when I had a temper and thought I was Superman. I screamed at the solders that we should get those guys, and one handed me his Uzi. That stopped me in my tracks, as I wasn't even sure where the trigger was. Then a soldier came up to me. He was from Chicago and in perfect English suggested I relax and sit down. The car was not destroyed and even if it was, who really cares. After all, it was manufactured in Germany! I sat.

It was three, perhaps four days later, about 5:30 in the morning, when I was awakened by a great deal of movement. The sister was very close to giving birth. They were upset that they had disturbed my sleep with the commotion, apologized and disappeared. I had not seen a hospital since I had been there. I dressed quickly and went out after them, only to be told that the hospital was near and she had walked there the last two times she was pregnant and about to give birth. "OK," I said, "But this time you don't need to walk, I'll drive everyone." They looked at me as if I were a mad man, smiled and continued walking. Frustrated, I just slowly drove alongside. I could feel the morning heat and knew it had to be affecting the soon-to-be third time mom, and the baby she was carrying. Finally, Ricky said something loudly that stopped them. Almost immediately they entered my car. I wish I could recall what it was she said, but it worked and that was the important thing.

The hospital was just over two miles away. Walking was lunacy, I thought. We entered and the ladies went into the one room available for surgery. In not more than a half an hour we heard the baby boy crying. I swear to you that the nurse went into a refrigerator and took out a cake! They played some music on a tape machine and we all danced with each other. I was in tears, in awe that I had played a part in this birth. Would the newborn have waited until his mother reached the hospital? Fortunately, we will never know.

They named the baby Moses, and Alon was chosen as his middle name. I was flattered. However, I felt uneasy suddenly. It was time to move on, which I did the next day, as you will see in the next story. I never saw Ricky again, but I did stop by the hospital to say goodbye to Moses Alon.

Addendum

My Volkswagen ended up in Miami Beach. But that's another story.

ISRAEL GOREN LEADS ME TO DR. WEISS, AND NOTHING IS EVER THE SAME

Oct. 17, 1965

While I was staying with Israel and Ora Goren in Elat, they noticed my back problems and made a phone call to Dr. Weiss, the man who had essentially performed a miracle in saving Ora's life. I was immediately invited to the man's house. He was almost 90 years old, with white hair. Not a line in his face, or on his body anywhere. Gruff, and not someone you take a liking to immediately. He was in fact unpleasant. The man told me to be quiet, and to follow him. He saw the canes and crutches I was using, and demanded that I LEAVE THEM AGAINST THE WALL. When I told him my problem, he said, "Your problem."

I made my way into his office, which was sparse, but did contain a number of pieces of equipment. He told me to take a seat and stare into his eyes. He then turned off all the lights in the room, except for the two strong spotlights that were on his desk. When I began to ask a question he told me to be quiet. There was nothing I could say to help myself. All he had was pen and paper. He started writing frantically. That continued for some considerable time. Eventually he stopped and said to me, "You recently had an operation on your spine. 4th and 5th vertebrae. Both of your legs were also affected." Then he said nothing, but just stared at me. I was stunned. I had told him nothing, and my friend Israel knew nothing of what had caused my pain and indisposition. Dr. Weiss then smirked and said, "I can help you!"

I was more than shocked, but I told him I would listen to every word. He said, "If you're serious this is what you will do. You will go to Elat, where you will sleep in a tent, where you will climb the red mountains, and swim in the sea. You will eat no animal flesh. For the first three weeks, you will eat only grapes. The next three weeks, you will have other fruits along with the grapes. The next three weeks, you will add vegetables." (By the time the fourth and final three weeks was to start, I reported to him that I was very hungry, so he allowed me to have the mix of fruits and vegetables in larger quantities.)

I remember that I was amazed hearing his words at this meeting. And it was then my turn to smirk. "You must be kidding! I can hardly walk."

He said, "Walk, that's your problem. And those pills you have, you will leave them with me. If you still think you need them when you get back, I will return them to you. You will leave your crutches here and I will return those, too, if you still think you need them."

I recall sitting back in my chair, staring at him, and taking his words in carefully. I decided there wasn't much of a choice, as every doctor I had visited, and there were a great many of them, gave me no hope of ever doing more than simply walking slowly. I knew it would be difficult, perhaps even an adventure, but I was ready to be healed. The next day I took my little Volkswagen and drove to Elat. About halfway there I saw a solider with a machine gun over her shoulder. I could tell it was a girl and did not hesitate to pull over for a chat. I made sure she saw the canes and crutches. That way she would know she could get away. I asked her where she was going and she said Elat. She told me her name was Ayella and I told her that was a pretty name. She said it meant "small deer." I said, "You mean like Bambi." She smiled and said, "Yes, you could say that."

She got in the car, and drove with me to Elat. We rented a tent, unpacked, and made ready for the activities that would soon take us over. Every day, morning, noon and night, with Bambi's help and that of others, I pushed myself. And I found myself soon accomplishing those demands that Dr. Weiss had placed on me.

The good doctor sent down grapes, bananas, all types of fruits and vegetables for his patients staying by the beach. My diet consisted of grapes only for the first three weeks, then different fruits along with grapes for the next three weeks, and then vegetables were added to the fruits for the next three weeks. The final three weeks I could add to the quantity of foods I consumed, but I was to have nothing other than fruits and vegetables.

I paid for nothing. It was all supplied by his people and the people who lived there. I lost about thirty pounds in the process. However, once back in "civilization," I regained most of it.

After about five or six months, Bambi had left for her unit. I stayed on a few more months with the help of friends. Afterwards, I went back to Haifa, where I stayed with the Gorens and helped work their farm.

About a week after I came back from Elat, I asked Israel to show me how to get back to Dr. Weiss's office. I wanted to thank him. I walked in, and said to his nurse, "I want to see Dr. Weiss." She asked if I had an appointment. I said, "No, but he will certainly see me." You can imagine the blush on my face when she said, "No appointment, no visit." I asked her to please talk to him — I just wanted two minutes. That's all I needed. She did so.

And Dr. Weiss came out to see me. He smiled when he saw I had recovered. He was friendly, but not overly.

I said, "You did it! You healed me. I'll always be grateful to you." He said he was pleased and hoped that he wouldn't have to see me again. I offered to pay him, but he refused. We shook hands. However, when I left his office, the nurse did let me know that Dr. Weiss could use a certain piece of equipment. I immediately ordered it and had it shipped to their office. It cost over $2,000. I never got a note of acknowledgement or thanks, but have always been glad I could help in some way with the work of this remarkable man.

I did see Dr. Weiss one more time, two years later. He asked how I was, and I told him I was fine, but a little weak. He suggested I add fish to provide protein I clearly needed. I added dairy at some point on my own, as the Gorens, total vegetarians, all ate dairy. I never touched meat or fowl again.

Ed. Note: Like the good doctor, Alon's face, at 70 years of age, has no lines.

FLAGS

As I mentioned, a few of us were going through the treatment at the beach together when I was healing through Dr. Weiss' regimen. The other patients were all roughly my age, and it was euphoric. Someone from the town nearby had given us Israeli flags; this was two years before Israel's 6 Day War with Egypt, and tensions were high. We got to talking around the fire one night — there was always a fire — and someone said, "We ought to go and stick these flags in Egypt's face!"

Two young men, one Algerian, one Swede, and I got up, took the flags and some diving clothing and plunged into the sea. We swam for what felt like a half an hour. We had a rope between us to keep us together. As soon as we saw the beach on the Egyptian side of the sea, we slithered ashore and planted the flags as deep as we could. It was on the way back that unfortunately one of the other fellows and I were bitten badly by fish. Someone said they were barracuda, but I don't believe it. Nevertheless, they cut into us. We bled, but made it back to our beach. There was a celebration planned, but once the group saw how seriously we were injured, that got postponed.

The next morning, two pilots from Beersheba came in by helicopter. One was a doctor who treated us, giving us medicine, bandages, and important information about how to handle the bites.

We then tried to celebrate, but the three of us were exhausted. To make matters worse, we had the pleasure of being greeted by the Israeli police. These gentlemen arrested us and placed our band of three in an Israeli police station. However, our friends made so much noise throughout the night, cheering for us, that we were given just a reprimand in the morning and let go with no further consequences.

EL CORDOBES AND SPAIN

I suppose it was the late 60's, when a few of us drove into Tijuana, Mexico. We were anxious to see the new super star of matadors, El Cordobes from Spain. Although none of us knew much about bullfighting, or even was thrilled by the idea, when there is an opportunity to see a greatly honored practitioner of almost any craft, some of us take advantage of it. And Cordobes was reputed to be one of the best of all time.

We stopped off first at the hotel in town for lunch. The waiter stated that the restaurant had invented the Caesar Salad. I have no idea if they really did, but it was extremely good. We noticed a full table of attractive men and women and I could tell by their accent they were from Spain, not Mexico. Various people came by to request an autograph from one man in particular. We quietly listened and realized it was El Cordobes himself. He had striking facial features and reminded me of the young actor Tyrone Power. I noticed his eyes. They were taking in everything all around him. When he saw me I gave a small smile and held up my glass to him. He surprised me by holding his glass up as well.

I called the waiter and told him to send both a glass of milk for Cordobes' strength, followed by a glass of champagne in celebration of success later today. The waiter delivered the message perfectly and it brought a volley of laughter from everyone with him.

After lunch the people at his table and mine waved a happy farewell and we were off to the stadium. Clearly I'm not a fan of this sport, although I do appreciate both the power the bulls have and the courage of those facing them in the ring. I never took the time, nor had the inclination to learn the intricate passes and many classical maneuvers and tactics that took place during these contests. I admit, however, that having met a renowned star, I was now somewhat intrigued by the plot of it. These animals weighed almost two thousand pounds, while the man in front of them usually came in at much less than two hundred. The matador would have to be swift and manipulate the bull in such a way that he would be in command. And there could be no hiding once they faced each other.

Once we were at the bullring, I had to admit that I loved the statuesque beauty and courage of the horses. I still recall the remark a man near me made, "When it is all done properly, it is a dance with a stunning finality. But when done poorly, it is barbaric." Before Cordobes there were two preliminary matadors. Both were business-like and seemed to be professional in their actions. I could have done without either. Then the trumpets sounded and the main attraction came out, resplendent in his shining suit of gold lights. He walked around the arena bowing gracefully to the thousands in attendance. A few minutes later the music played louder, and out from a corner came a beast so large that I was stunned.

This match was so different from the first two. Almost a ballet, and there was almost absolute silence. The bull charged and it was astonishing how close the horns came to the matador. Finally, after tantalizing the crowd a bit longer, Cordobes withdrew his sword, and in seconds it was over. It was so quick, almost bloodless. After a few seconds of total awe, the audience stood and screamed El Cordobes' name as he bowed and made his exit.

I felt as if I were perhaps in ancient Rome when the gladiators fought. But that was one man against another; this was so very different. The other two matadors made another appearance, each doing what they were supposed to. They were both forgettable. Then it was the second and final turn of Cordobes. The entire audience stood to pay homage to him. He wore a silver suit this time that picked up the demise of the sun as shadows appeared. When they opened the gate for his opponent, the hush of the people in the crowd was almost frightening. If the other bull was thick in its muscle, this one was colossal! These animals are raised from birth to do this, but this was more elephant than bull, with very long horns, and he raced across the stadium at incredible speed. The silence was deafening. The two met in the center of the ring. Cordobes brandished his cape as if it were a magic wand. This was no ordinary animal. He was huge and seemed to gain strength as he was learning about the man in front of him. Suddenly the magnificent creature stopped his attack, and turned his head. A horn went into the Matador's leg, and as if he had gored a chicken the bull lifted Cordobes up off his feet and swung him high in the air. The crowd was stunned. The two other fighters who had taken part earlier raced to help him. The bull attacked them and they ran, but that gave Cordobes time to retrieve his weapon, which had gone flying away. His own people yelled for him to get out. The red blood on the silver suit was almost a shock. Instead, he dusted himself off and called TORO, TORO. The animal charged and somehow hit only the cape, not the man holding it. This game of life continued for perhaps ten minutes longer. How Cordobes stood on one leg while evading the horns was amazing. Then the bull stopped. He was soaked in sweat and obviously exhausted. Cordobes stunned all of us when he calmly approached it, and petted the bull's forehead. The toreadors on horseback rode hard to place their long lances into the animal, who had just raised his head, awaiting certain death. Incredibly, Cordobes waved them off. He had made the decision to allow the bull to live, and it slowly left the arena. People stood and cheered as if they had witnessed a rebirth. A stretcher was brought out and the wounded but proud matador was carried off waving at everyone, a scene never to be forgotten.

Not quite the ending. After our visit to the bullring, our party left and found that the traffic was terrible. Rather than fight it, we went back to the hotel. All of us almost tingled with excitement. We ordered food and wine and could not stop speaking of the events in the ring. Then it happened. On a crutch, El Cordobes, now showered, bandaged, looking worn out but pleased, came in. Everyone stood in admiration and he smiled broadly. At some point I approached him and after giving congratulations, mentioned I was to be in Spain in a few months. Of course he was just being courteous, but said that if I were near his town to stop in and say hello. Naturally, I agreed. A few months later, friends and I were driving through Cordobes' area of Spain and I asked at my hotel if he lived nearby. Imagine my surprise when I was told his ranch was only a half hour away. Being young and full of myself I insisted we go. My friends and I found it easily and soon were at his front door. He was paged and I reminded him of that day, and that he had invited me to visit if in the area. Obviously, I thought he would not, but he was extremely kind and took us for a tour. He looked at me and asked if I was ready was to try my luck. With a calf, of course, not with a bull. So it was arranged. That little calf with no horns knocked me down over and over. Everyone had a good laugh at my expense. We went back to Cordobes' hacienda and he invited us for a late lunch. It was during that time he stood up, laughed and left the room. No one had a clue what was happening. A few moments later he reappeared holding two glasses, both of which he handed to me. One had milk in it, the other champagne. I have no idea how, but he had remembered.

SCIENTOLOGY ... 1968
MOM AND ME

My good friend Gary Engel, whom I met when I was about 15 years old, had a charming father, Howie. It was said his father owned 10% of the Dunes Hotel in Las Vegas, the Hotel Nacional in Havana, and that he had interests in others as well. There were various rumors about him, because he looked, dressed and spoke like a cross between Jimmy Cagney and Edward G. Robinson. Like his father, who was active in the organization, Gary was into L. Ron Hubbard and Scientology. In fact, Scientology attracted many young people who were searching for "something." They came and paid a lot of money to hear Gary's father, even to read his words.

The week after meeting Howie, I went to a symposium of his on Scientology. Purely as a lark, I wrote a few pages of advertising for them. They were impressed, and asked me to cover all their written publicity. When I looked disinterested, they said they were a bit short on funds, but would provide me with thousands of dollars of free classes. I still hesitated and they upped the ante. I could even bring another person. I agreed!

I ran this past the most sensible person I knew, my mother. Her first thoughts were that I was joking, had smoked some funny weeds or had a touch of the flu. But I convinced her that a few nights a week could be enjoyable and interesting. She agreed, based on that.

We drove down to the ORG, as it was known. The building was somewhat imposing, like a large school. We met with the leaders I had seen the day before. They were full of kind words about how pleased they were to enlighten the two of us, even if they were not charging an actual fee. Eventually they indicated it was clear that we wished to learn more. So, Mom and I were directed into separate rooms, each having an "Auditor," their word for someone who was about to run through a selected list of questions for the potential new recruit. You sit opposite this person holding two "E-meters," one in each hand. Basically, they were fancy tin cans with wires connected to a machine that informs the Auditor if you are replying truthfully or not. A primitive lie detector, it somehow is supposed to provide the truth underlying your reply.

I recall being asked if I were comfortable. I answered, "Not really. This chair is a bit hard." "Thank you," I was told. These were the two words always said after each answer I gave. Never "Wrong" or "Right," or "Good," or "Let's do that again." Just "Thank you." I was asked if I liked the room itself. I looked around and again said, "Not really. It could use a paint job, and that picture looks like it came from a thrift shop." "Thank you."

The questions continued for about 20 minutes. Then suddenly my auditor stood and said, "Oh, my! You have cleared Level One, in the fastest time I've ever recorded." I was bemused, as all I did was reply to simple questions with honest answers. I thanked him and went into the hall, where I saw my mother. She had cleared Level One a few minutes before I did. I went to the main office and advised them of what had just taken place. The senior people came out full of admiration for us. I said that we should continue on. "So soon?" he replied, "You're not tired?" I assured him we were both fine and would very much like to continue on to Level Two. They had a meeting and arrangements were made with different people, E-Meters, and even rooms. Level Two went almost exactly like the first; a few minutes longer as there were more questions. However, absolutely no difficulties for either of us. Again, there was jubilation from the Leaders that our times were simply marvelous.

When I asked to go on to Level Three, together they declined. Different Auditors needed to be brought in for that, and preparations had to be made. But if we were back next week, we could do it. I said then I would wait until that time before I turned in some new writing. After a meeting amongst themselves they said that they would see to it that it could take place in two nights. I pushed hard and said that I would be disappointed if they did not have Level Four prepared for us as well. Their skepticism was a joy to look upon. However, they agreed.

Needless to say, Levels Three and Four went only a bit longer, again without any difficulties. They were stunned, as it seemed like we were breaking all records. What remained were the fearful Level Five and the seldom attainable CLEAR! We were told that only a few reached those levels without a great deal of work. That meant taking numerous classes that were intense and would need to be paid for. Bless my mother for not laughing. This was Psychiatry Inspection Analysis 101 at its wretched, inferior worst.

Nevertheless, I turned in some advertising writing they loved, and they wanted much more.

It was agreed that the following Wednesday we would attempt the almost impossible. If we could survive Level Five, they would have the special Auditors there to allow us to attempt to go CLEAR! My only surprise was Mom's comment to me in the car that she wasn't certain she wanted to return. She had earlier referred to it as a "Kindergarten" for those that simply could not face the realities of life. She wasn't totally comfortable telling a stranger private issues in her life and especially now that she was a widow. I answered that she would not know the individual speaking to her and likely would never see him or her again. It was only the truth that was required. Because so many people think they have so much to hide, they retain it inside. That's unhealthy and is an avoidance of reality. She only looked at me and smiled. I said I would collect her at 5:00 p.m. She said, "That will be just fine. After we become CLEAR, you can take me out to a nice dinner. But that will be the end of my kindergarten classes." I agreed.

We were given some challenges on our return. Totally separated. Auditors with attitudes and no welcoming faces on anyone. We both skated Level Five, no problems. These Scientologists who had been so friendly, now wore different looks. We were then led onto a balcony with still more new people and dark rooms. But they made a major mistake, as they allowed us to see each other for a brief moment. Just enough time to give a one-eyed wink to each other. Any doubts in our minds were immediately erased. We were ready.

Later they hugged us and said that it was amazing for a mother and son to have achieved CLEAR so quickly, and on the same evening. In fact, never done. Mom did me proud and did not crack up laughing.

Addendum: Friend Gary Engel vanished from Las Vegas and no one there has ever heard from him again. Bennett Orr, another friend attending, jumped overboard from the Scientology Org ship in Athens when they would not return his passport. He was fished out, given his passport, and worked out a new situation, he thought, with the Scientology Org ship. No one has ever seen him again either.

L. Ron Hubbard? That science fiction writer couldn't write a better book than the one in this story.

VANISHED!
Episode 1

In April 1968, my brother Steve bought a new green (my least favorite color) Triumph sports car in London. We went to get it and decided to take a drive before shipping it back to America. We drove through England into Dover to catch a ship to France. After we'd gone to bed, the police came to the door and woke us up. It seems that someone had stolen our luggage rack off the rear of the vehicle, and the police had noticed that the car had been damaged. We never found the rack, and although my brother was repaid by insurance, it was a nuisance.

Nevertheless, we had all our things with us in the room, and could proceed without the luggage container. We headed toward Switzerland where I had a girlfriend whose father owned a watch factory. While we were driving through a lovely small town, I asked Steve to pull over. I had seen a small charming bank, and on the spot decided to get one of those famous Swiss numbered bank accounts starting with the one hundred dollars extra I had on hand. Upon entering I was greeted by a friendly lady who offered her assistance. She told me a numbered account required a minimum of ten thousand dollars. It seems I was only nine thousand nine hundred short of that figure. She was very pleasant and didn't make fun of my shortfall. We still opened the account, but under my name, with one hundred dollars.

For a few years I received statements from the bank and then they couldn't be contacted whenever I tried. In the 1970's when I moved to London, I had an opportunity to visit the area. Gone! The bank had vanished. I visited other branches but they all said they had no idea what or where I was speaking of and in minutes those conversations were over. To this day the fortune that my hundred invested dollars represented has never been heard of again.

VANISHED!
Episode 2

Later in the trip we were driving back to Paris and the rain was extremely heavy. When we spotted a small but very well situated hotel on the side of the road, we were all grateful, and Steve pulled into their parking lot.

It took only a few minutes for us to learn that room prices were very reasonable, and a buffet dinner was being served for about three dollars. We parked, took separate $4 rooms and feasted on marvelous food. Excellent local French wine was included. As we dined on our succulent meals, we also enjoyed a piano player who sang in various languages.

It was after midnight when we bid the hotelier, pianist and the rest of our party au revoir and good night. In the sunlight of the morning we came down for a breakfast; huge and delicious. Steve looked at the car and was astonished that it had been washed and there was no charge for that. Not even a tip. We looked at each other as we drove off, knowing we had found a wonderful special place.

I've been in that town since many times. Steve has also revisited it. No one, and I do mean no one recalls the hotel. It simply never existed. Had Steve not been with me I would think it was some sort of hallucination. But he still has the receipt that no one there can explain.

There used to be a TV series called "The Twilight Zone." We now believe we have been there.

SAN FRANCISCO, CALIFORNIA ... 1969

I was "Head Hunted," and persuaded that it would be good for me financially to move from Los Angeles to San Francisco. The opportunity was alluring — I would play a major role in the building, marketing and basically all parts of a project known as "Bull Pine Ranch," a top secret underground facility that would eventually house some thousands of so-called important people. They would form the brain trust of American industries in the event of an attack on the country. Who would actually select the people that would be admitted I had no idea. However, I knew I would not be one of them, not one of those allowed to survive. Many expressed a good deal of interest, but not one company had come forth yet to become a tenant in this project based on doom...

But I'm ahead of myself. Moving from southern California to the Bay Area at first did not please me. I wasn't comfortable with all the protests taking place in San Francisco regarding the Viet Nam war. So I looked outside the city proper, driving over to Marin County on the Golden Gate Bridge. The crossing itself was a joy at the time, but later it became an everyday occurrence. Once in Marin, I bought the local newspapers and went to brokers who bought, sold, and rented properties in the area. Then I discovered Mill Valley. It was a gorgeous place with trees everywhere, no large super stores, and nice people. Almost set in wilderness, with wildlife even. Luck was with me. I found a wonderful A-frame home, rather high in the hills, with a timber deck all around it, and a wood burning fireplace. Quiet, rustic, and simply lovely and warm.

Although it was only for a year, when I moved up to Mill Valley from L.A. I had shipped all my possessions: furniture, art, books, TV, major stereo system, everything. The movers brought it all into my rented A-frame house in the mountains, in its nature-filled, private setting. I put my belongings all in place over the next few days. There were some personal papers that I had left in L.A., so I flew back for two days.

On my return I was stunned — I had been burglarized. A great deal was missing that was important. I sat down, and almost immediately the phone rang. The voice was calm and very precise. "Hello, sir. Welcome back. It was my friends and I that took your things. Please listen carefully. You can easily purchase them from us in perfect condition. We will require $700 in cash. You simply have to go downtown, and be at the bus station at 8:00 p.m. with the money. You need to know we have done this many times and one of us is a policeman. So if you call or go to them, I assure you that you will never see your belongings again. Also, once this transaction is completed your home will never again be visited by us or anyone else, as this is our territory. Go to the bus station and sit on a bench. Wear jeans and a white shirt. A girl will approach you and ask for an envelope. You give it to her with the money inside and go to one of the local restaurants or cafés. After 11:00 p.m., return to your home, where you will see all your things. This is not a large amount of money and you will not be displeased that the transaction was completed, since you will receive everything back."

My temper was boiling but suppose everything he said was correct? He then said that he understood if I was angry, however all I had to do was go to my neighbors' homes on either side, and they would substantiate everything. I said I will do exactly that. He replied he would call back in half an hour.

I went out and was able to speak with one of the families a few doors down that happened to be home. They had children and I was comfortable they were not the people who had created this mess. They said the only home not hit was the one on the block that was owned by Janis Joplin, who was on tour. They were also able to negotiate a better price than demanded. I went home, not certain what to do.

The voice called in exactly half an hour and asked if I was satisfied. I had checked my wallet and told him the truth. That I had exactly $492.00 and I was prepared to give him $475.00 as I needed money for gas and did not want to be without any funds. I heard him speak with others. He was almost laughing and said that they could tell by my things, I was not a wealthy person. It was hardly worth their time, but they would go along with me. As far as the extra money, they may be thieves, but they were good people. As long as I never made a report, I could consider it a housewarming gift. As it was getting dark, I should immediately dress as he said and go to the bus station. "Welcome to Mill Valley" were his last words. I changed into jeans and a white shirt, drove the mile or so to the bus station and found a bench to sit on. In about 10 minutes a young girl who looked about 15 years old approached me smiling, and asked if I had an envelope. I took a good long look at her so that if it was just a further robbery, I could describe her. She took the envelope, smiled and said, "Welcome to Mill Valley!"

I slowly walked to a pleasant café nearby, wanting to tell someone, anyone this story. But I decided to play the game, and had a lonely meal. I walked until 11:00 p.m., and drove to my house, not knowing what to expect. When I walked in the front door I was amazed. Everything seemed to be back and they had even plugged in the TV and stereo. A few minutes later the phone rang. It was the voice again, asking if I was satisfied that everything was there and in no worse condition. Everything was and I found myself actually thanking him.

I spent the next year there without any unpleasant incidents. I did tell this about a month later to a detective in L.A. I had met. He listened intently and said I did the correct thing. I was awed by his reply. I asked, "What about LAW AND ORDER?" He just shrugged and said that apparently, this was my entrance fee to Mill Valley. I moved to London shortly later and never heard if these thieves but "good people" were ever caught. Another mystery in life.

ONLY IN MILL VALLEY

One evening I remember I was driving to my new home, along what was basically a one car road, a stretch of unpaved dirt along which another vehicle had to pull over to let another pass. Suddenly I noticed a Mercedes behind me, driving a bit too fast, and erratically. I pulled over and it swept past me. I thought it a bit odd, as this road ended in a sort of a cul de sac. Mine was the second home before the end. I drove into my open garage and was a bit surprised to see the Mercedes very slowly hit the wall of the garage next door, and more than once. The driver simply was not fully together, and was smashing up the car. I took a deep breath and went over. A rather hippy-looking young woman sat behind the wheel. I excused myself and offered to drive the car into her garage for her. She looked at me, closed her eyes and said, "Yes, please, Officer." I just smiled and said, "I'm not a cop, just your new next door neighbor." I could smell what she had been smoking and had a little laugh as I drove my first Mercedes Benz, even if it was only a few feet. When I'd got her car into her garage, I walked the woman to her door and said, "Have a nice sleep."

About 8:00 p.m. the bell rang and I was more than a little surprised. When I opened it, it was the Mercedes girl. By the way, Mercedes was what I called her the entire year I knew her. She had a bottle of pretty good wine and said she had come to offer apologies. We had a few minutes of small talk and she offered to share the wine with me. I had hardwood floors, a marvelous music center and even a barber chair amongst many other bits and pieces on the floors and walls. She felt comfortable enough amid my belongings to light up another one of her favorite cigarettes, which I declined, in order to savor the wine without any distractions.

When "Mercedes" had come in, I was playing an album from the blues era. She stood and proceeded to sing along with it. That's when I knew for certain Janis Joplin had come home from her tour — this was indeed the lady herself. I went to my albums and pulled out every one she had ever made, and then took out other wonderful artists from the current time and earlier eras. Some she said she had never heard of.

I cooked a meal, which Janis appreciated and needed, and we had another bottle of wine. She was not a good looking lady; the drink and drugs were already taking their toll. But her laugh was infectious, and her gift of loving the moment could only have been born by someone who had been through a great deal. We bonded that evening.

In the morning we just looked at each other. She was a bit alarmed for a reason I never asked. But I smiled, laughed and told her that her next door neighbor would always be happy to feed her. It broke the ice and she was pleased. We became very close neighbors.

She was on the road a lot doing concerts and I attended many of them, almost always paying full price to sit in one of the first three rows, which upset her. Then I'd tell she was worth it, and the arguing would end. During the shows Janis would spot me and sing some of the songs directly at me. She was so much a bigger than life character I doubted anyone guessed there was a relationship between us, and always acted as if I were just the guy she chose to sing to that evening.

I was seeing other "normal" ladies, and Janis and I each did our own thing, but there were special times. With her, it wasn't love, it was respect for each other that made the relationship work.

I met big Brother and the Holding Company, her band, a few days after I first met Janis. They were very good except they didn't like or trust me. In their eyes I looked like the police. I understood their feelings — in the 60's drugs were a happening thing. But I was a guy just making a living, preparing to move to Europe, and return to school, and had a different image to portray. Janis knew this and stood up for me, which I truly appreciated. Eventually a few of her friends visited my home and barriers came down.

* * *

Where I lived in Mill Valley was wonderful. The weather was often lovely, though there were also many days when it was damp and cold. Chilly days served to start me on a new creative path. The cold drove me indoors, and I began to experiment with cooking. Much to my delight, the art of creating food became a true pleasure.

It wasn't long after I began learning to cook that Janis and her group and some of my own friends came for free hot meals, and of course lots of wine. There were two instances I remember when Janis and members of her group gave private concerts for us. She just called them rehearsals, but they were magical.

* * *

As if it were yesterday, I remember being at home and starting to walk up the staircase to my office, when the voice of the disc jockey on the jazz radio station I always listened to came on air. "I have to interrupt to tell you that Janis Joplin was found dead of an overdose of drugs in Hollywood tonight." I fell onto the steps in tears. Shattered, I just sat there and wept for what seemed forever. I couldn't believe she would do that to herself; just a few days earlier she was so happy and making plans for a tour. For at least the previous eight months, to my knowledge, Janis had not been taking heroin.

To this day I believe that Janis was murdered. A police cover up? No, I simply think she wasn't important enough yet for them to look into it. Forty years later I still think about her, and grieve. This world has lost such a great talent.

Some months after I learned of Janis' death, I was heading to Europe as planned. As I boarded the flight to London, she appeared in my mind's eye before any other image or thought had a chance to make itself known.

A very special lady. I wish you could have known her.

TEMPLE DRAKE

Chicago in the summer is warm, and there are times when a cold brew comes in handy. In one of those moments, as I was walking down Rush Street, my throat felt parched and I happened to spy what looked like a decent pub. The place probably was, but it's the customers that can change one's emotions rather quickly. A few steps before me a young lady with a marvelous figure was entering the premises. We walked in almost together and she ordered a cold drink. The jukebox was playing and it felt like a good place to be. I was certainly wrong.

It wasn't five minutes before a bloated man at the end of the bar said loudly, "I know you. You're that stripper with the snake at the Kit Kat Club." She ignored him and the bartender told him to watch what he was saying. He stood and walked to the jukebox and put some coins in.

"Come on, baby, give us a show!"

She continued to ignore the boor and looked at the elderly bartender for some help. He was now having none of it and walked away. As the burly man approached her, she told him in no uncertain terms to leave her alone. He grabbed her hair hard, she screamed and I moved quickly and hit him a few times before he went down. That's when I saw a pistol in a holster on his belt. I dropped a few dollars on the bar, grabbed her and we were out the door.

We must have run two streets when she stopped and said, "That cop won't run this far in his condition. Why did you help me?" First I had to take in the point that the guy was a detective, then I simply said that I didn't like ladies being attacked. She smiled and replied that in fact she really was no lady, she was the exotic dancer he was talking about. We chatted for a few moments and she hailed a taxi. "You never had that beer and I have a few in my refrigerator. My treat."

She lived in one of those buildings you can rent by the month. Not fancy, but clean and even with a doorman out front. The apartment was a decent size for one person and I soon learned she had a closet filled with wigs on top, g-strings on hangers and very high heeled shoes on the bottom. I was in a new world. She handed me a beer and started to undress. I told her that it wasn't necessary, but she only smiled and replied that she always paid her debts. I decided not to argue the point.

Later, I could tell she was hungry and tired and could use a meal and a bit of rest. I cooked up some concoction. About an hour later she awoke, amazed that I was still there and had cooked a meal as well. I suppose it was about then that we realized we actually liked each other. It turned into a very pleasant evening. She told me a bit about her life and I did the same. However, we both held back quite a bit. She was fun. We laughed and enjoyed the time together. Later she said she had to go to work and hoped I would understand. I said it was no problem and that I looked forward to seeing her again. She smirked and said that she really wasn't a "nice" girl. I laughed and could only say, "Great!"

About midnight I dressed and caught a cab to the Kit Kat Club. I was expecting the worst but was pleased. It was a major upscale club in a decent area. I took a seat at a small table just as Temple came on stage. There was the snake, but it was made of rubber and part of her act. She was very professional and I assume did all the moves that these performers do. When she saw me she actually stopped and smiled. Of course I was pleased. I have an ego as well. Later she introduced me backstage by my first name, because neither of us knew our full names, or if they were even real. Being backstage in a dressing room for strippers was quite an idea eye opener. Especially for a young man.

I spent some weeks in Chicago and was with her almost every night. It was quite an experience. This was the 60's and I was growing up fast. Coincidence happened when she was offered a headline act in New Orleans. Much more money. A few days later I was offered a position in either Atlanta or…yes, New Orleans. My choice.

We took an apartment for a month but she said that this job came with "other conditions." I could guess what they were. She always made it clear that she needed money.

I had no idea why it was so important that she required so much and never asked. I suppose it was the second or third night that she

came in very late. She asked that I not touch her, showered and came to bed. After a few minutes I heard her whimper.
"Tell me," I asked. Then I saw the bruise on her face and I got irate. The only word I then said was "WHY?" I had no idea why she was putting herself in harm's way.

Then it poured out. Tommy, it's all about Tommy! She had a son, with Cerebral Palsy. The best place for his continuous care was at an institution in Georgia. But it was $700 dollars a week. She had no insurance. That money would include all medication, clothing and 24 hour loving care. Tommy was all she cared for in life. If she had to sell her body, so be it.

She visited him every three months and I asked to go with her the next time. We flew there and they had a limo meet us. I thought that odd but said nothing. The place was large and looked like a school. There were some workers' building a swimming pool. Temple dressed conservatively from head to toe. Hardly a speck of make-up. She could have passed almost as a nun. I wore a suit and tie. An attractive lady took us to the head office where we met Mr. Ferguson. He was a bit overweight, dapper in dress with a thin mustache. I never liked those things. I always felt a man looked sneaky wearing one. It didn't take me long to realize Mr. Ferguson was hiding behind his.

Tommy was brought in and I thought he looked scrawny, thin and simply not very healthy. He didn't recognize Temple, which she had told me would be the case. She held him and tried hard to compose herself. I asked to see his room which Mr. Ferguson wasn't too happy about, but I persisted and we went — Tommy, Temple and a so-called nurse. Tommy looked a bit spaced and I was troubled by that. When we went into the room I asked to use the bathroom which did not please the lady at all, but I went anyway. It was dirty with toilet rolls lined up on the floor. I opened the medicine cabinet and was stunned by all the vials of tablets.

None had his name on it, but there were Valium, Xanax and others that I could not see a youngster taking. Worst of all, there was no lock on the cabinet door. I called the woman in and inquired about all this. She looked frightened and said Mr. Ferguson would answer any questions we had. The answer he gave was that on occasion patients needed to be sedated for fear they were having a spell and could hurt themselves. The reason his name was not on the labels was they bought through direct purchase and that kept the costs down. To maintain an institution was very expensive. He was lying and he knew I saw through it.

I asked about the pool and he said that with close supervision it could be a form of exercise. They would be building a fence around it, to protect the patients. We had an early dinner there and I was surprised to see steak and vegetables. He showed us various menus that looked as if they came from a restaurant. Temple kept looking at me. She could sense that I was unhappy about a number of issues. Later we said our goodbye's and I shook his limp, sweaty hand. She and I hardly spoke until we were on the plane. That's when I told her that I intended to look into that institution. I thought she might object, but she didn't. Suddenly she wasn't so comfortable there either.

I went back to Chicago where I asked a lawyer friend for his assistance. When I went back to my hotel there were a number of messages there for me. Almost all from Temple. I called and she was almost hysterical. It seems Tommy climbed the pool fence and drowned. I recalled that he needed assistance just walking. He could never have climbed a fence. Mr. Ferguson had called with the bad news and said he would refund her money for the balance of that term. The body would be sent to wherever she wished and they would cover those costs, as they were all grieving as well and as a sign of good faith.

I flew back the next day, but first I met the lawyer and filled him in. Although he obviously did not know Tommy, he was furious. He made calls and finally was told of a lawyer in Georgia that was excellent. More calls were made and I was ecstatic. The next week was almost a blur. Temple and I met the lawyer at his office and he offered to take the case without charge. He immediately contacted Ferguson and told him his offer was rejected and if necessary he would take this to the Governor and the Board of Health. Ferguson panicked and offered one hundred thousand dollars. I thought Temple would pass out. "That's an insult!" the lawyer screamed. "One million is more like it. Have your lawyer call me now or I will do all in my power to shut you down." About 20 minutes passed and he was marvelous. The other attorney called and tried to settle the matter with a two hundred thousand dollar offer. They went back and forth. The bank was called and Ferguson made calls to friends. Temple looked faint and I took her down the hall. She was still in shock over Tommy, but now money was going to go to her. More than she ever imagined. On the verge of tears she sat on a chair and asked me to deal with it. I reminded her of that night she returned from the club and how she had suffered. I said that if we can make the right deal, she could give up that life forever. It would be a gift from Tommy to you. She started crying and a secretary came to assist her. Five hundred and forty thousand dollars was every penny that they could come up with. The lawyer said if we took them to court we could likely get more, but that would take time. I sat with him and we worked out that with no payments for Tommy and bank interest, Temple would have enough funds that she need never work again. She would certainly not be wealthy, but she would be comfortable. We made the deal.

Temple wanted to go into nursing specializing in children with disabilities. I saw her only once after that and she had almost gotten over her son's passing. She was even looking a bit matronly. As a gift to me, she gave me the fake snake she had used in her stage act. We laughed and later really rejoiced, when we heard

Ferguson's so-called healing institution had been closed down. He was facing criminal charges on a number of counts.

I said "Tommy didn't die in vain." I gave her a last hug, picked up my new pet, a fake snake, and never saw or heard from Temple Drake again. You see she had gone back to her real name. I never knew what it was.

RINGALIVIO.....THE GAME OF LIFE

I suppose this was about 1968 or '69. The Hollywood Hills. None other than Liberace lived across the street in his mansion. He and I would exchange pleasantries from time to time. But I was never in his house. Thinking back, I'm rather sorry about that.

One day my friend Ron came over, as we had some film to develop. A few months earlier I had purchased a large kit, with an enlarger and all the trays and miscellaneous items that were required to take film and turn it into pictures that hopefully people would enjoy. Just an occasional hobby that was harmless, or so we thought......

There was a knock on the door and we smiled with the thought that his fiancé and my mother had arrived early. That turned out to be far from reality. We opened the door to be met by two young strangers, both holding guns.

"GET IN AND HURRY!" they shouted.

I was concerned as I could immediately see they were high on something. Also, I was not certain of Ron's attitude. He was smiling and almost jovial about it. The door was slammed shut and we were told to get on the floor. That's when Ron said, "OK, OK, the game's over. I'm not about to lie down on the floor."

It was obvious that he thought that I knew these two and was playing a practical joke. He could not have been more mistaken. As I tried to advise him of that, one of them struck him and forced him to the floor. He quickly caught on to the fact that this was real and I knew no more than he did. They screamed for money. I calmly said that the only funds I had were in my pocket and that I assumed my friend was in a similar position. They were now speaking in Spanish and talking about my television and other items.

"Guns. Where are your guns?" one of them asked me. I lied and said we had none and were only developing pictures. One of them was extremely shaky and I was about to try and go for him. But then Ron said, "Well, Ollie, this is a fine mess you got me into!," and gave me a look that said please don't try anything foolish.

One of the two thugs ripped the telephone cord from the wall and wrapped it around Ron's hands and feet. The other man tied electrical tape to my wrist and ankles. These were two young, but certainly dangerous men, and that concerned me greatly. In their present drugged state they could do anything. Now Ron and I were both on the floor, with jackets thrown over our heads. The front door opened and I heard the men start to take my belongings out. I was not clear about what their "final" intentions with us would be. Then an idea caught hold. I started to laugh loudly. As I had hoped, this confused them. Ron thought I had lost my mind. "Guys," I said. "Don't you know you're doing me a big favor? I have insurance." (Actually I didn't, but how were they to know?) "You see, when the police come, I'll give them different descriptions of you, they will write up their report and I will collect twice what those things you're taking actually cost me. Gracias, amigos....tonight we all make money!"

The tall skinny one with a badly pockmarked face kicked me in the ribs and said he liked my humor and way of thinking. I told him to come back in a few months and we could do it again. They laughed and left casually.

Somehow, and I have no idea to this day how, I managed to break the tape that bound my wrists. Then I quickly undid the tape around my feet. I could hear the thieves arranging everything in their van, and moved as quickly as possible to my bedroom. There, under my dress shirts was my Beretta pistol with a box of shells. With them in hand I raced up the stairs to the street and started to shoot as the van pulled away. To this very moment I have no idea if even one bullet was successful. It was about 9:00 p.m., I was wearing socks, jeans and a T-shirt and holding a gun that was firing shells at those two young men I considered very dangerous. There was no question but that the crack of each bullet was heard in dozens of homes.

Just then a car pulled up behind me. I turned around, prepared to glare at the occupants, with unpleasant intentions. In actual fact, what happened next *was* somewhat unpleasant. My mother and Ron's fiancé were the people in the car. Obviously, there were raised voices, concern, fear, and questions. Where and how was Ron? Why was I holding a pistol, and who was I shooting at? The young lady ran down the steps to see if Ron was alive and well. I smiled at my mother and she said simply, "Why is it always you?" Then she asked if I was OK, which made me laugh. I would have thought that would have been her first question.

In a few moments Ron and his girl came up the steps shaking their heads in disbelief. We called the police and explained the evening to them. They pulled me aside and said that those two could return and next time I should not be so civil, and should start shooting at them from the outset. I thanked them for their advice and a few weeks later moved to San Francisco.

Epilogue: I understand Ron's wedding was pleasant. I couldn't attend as I was already living in Europe. Shortly later he and his wife had twin daughters, Cindy and Carrie. Yes, those of you who know me now realize that I am married to Carol, the fiancée in the car with my mother.

LATE 60'S -1970'S

Top: "Like Sleeping on a Cloud"
Western Waterbeds Van

Below: Alon celebrates
Grand Opening of the company,
Precursor to Western Medical Group,
with girls ... and two male staff members

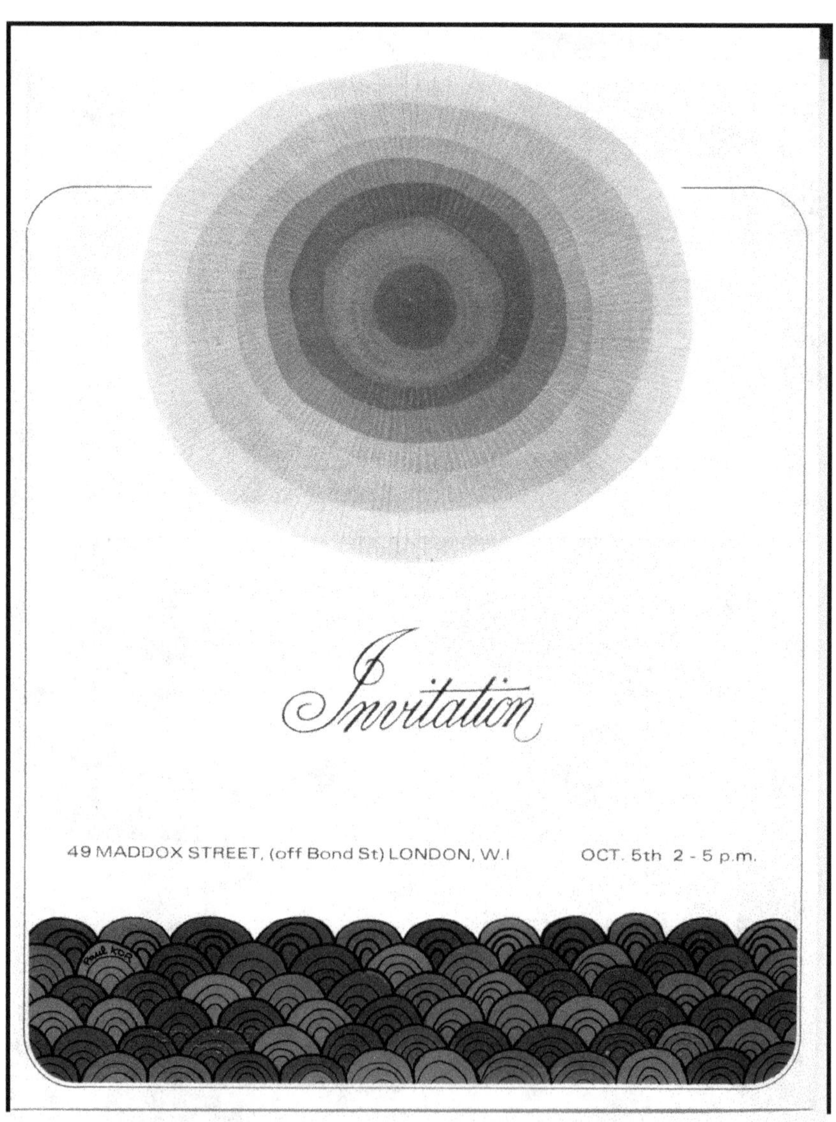

Invitation to the Grand Opening of Western Medical

FROM CHICAGO TO EUROPE

I got into trouble with a vending company one time, but I got out of it. This story began when I went in with my bodyguard, Mike Haig, to a coffee shop that had a number of my machines. We saw that one of ours had been placed out back, and a competitor's machine stood in its place. Mike and I picked up the offending piece of equipment, took it out back, and put ours back inside where it belonged.

The manager didn't know how to handle this. I told him to call the competing company and explain what had just transpired. They immediately dispatched two fellows right out of the Sopranos. Mike and I were young and in shape. A fight ensued, which we ended quickly.

"Take us to your president," we ordered. They agreed, but before we went out I made two phone calls to friends, gave them the address we were going to, and told my friends to meet us there with a number of other pals. We then left the coffee shop, following the two goombahs.

They led us into the vast chamber that housed the offices of the company as well as its equipment. There sat a squat, hairy, balding who looked like Bob Hoskins. He immediately was furious with me and made all sorts of threats. There were at least twenty-five of his employees there. I directed Mike to go outside. The boss paid no attention. Mike went out and returned with perhaps forty of our friends, many carrying baseball bats and car chains. The boss finally became civilized. He sat down and we had a long talk. He agreed not to take any of my locations, and I agreed to reciprocate.

Two days later I received a phone call from Delbert Coleman, the chairman and president of Seaburg Enterprises. They made all the jukeboxes in the world, and they are still the world's leader in the field. He requested that I fly to Chicago to meet with him and talk. I got him to offer a first class ticket and two days later flew to the windy city for the first time in my life.

The first thing Del did when we met was to make me an offer I couldn't refuse. He bought out my vending company for a marvelous figure, and then offered me a top salary to join his company. It seemed that Del was organizing a team of young, tough men to visit distributors throughout America. Their job would be to help when there were physical difficulties forced upon his distributors. Team members would be sent in packs of two each, one to watch the other's back. My partner was Joey Frisina. He was about 6'3", 220 pounds. We became fast friends. Two years later I even went to his wedding in L.A.

Joey and I were sent to a number of places, the last one being Houston, Texas, where a competitor of Seaburg took shots at our car. I'm sure they missed on purpose because they were right alongside of us. But it was enough to concern us, and we called Del, who immediately ordered us to leave Houston and go to New Orleans. He would send a bigger team to Houston, about seven guys.

In about a year's time, our contracts were up. Del offered some of the men positions with the company. When it came to me, he offered me a very special job. When you update the equipment in any of your customer's places of business, you take back the machines they had before. For some reason, he chose me to move out all the used equipment. At first I wasn't very excited. Until he said, "You'll have to move to Europe to do it."

He was aware of the fact that I had been to Europe on a number of occasions, and that I felt comfortable there. I flew to Brussels two weeks later and in a short time went to Paris, London, even

Morocco. Within seven months every bit of used equipment Seaburg had was sold, and I was out of a job.

Del wanted me to come back to Chicago to work for him, but I was so enamored of Europe that I decided to stay on for an indeterminate amount of time. I would cross whatever bridge I came to.

THE BEGINNING OF WESTERN MEDICAL LONDON....APRIL 1971

Although I was never a strict believer in "fate," this incident may have converted me. It was after 7:00 p.m. and pouring rain, on a very nasty, dark London evening. The streets were almost empty and most people had gone home. My showroom and offices were absent any human life, and I was only there catching up on some paperwork. I thought the front door was locked, but the last person out forget to lock it. Fortunately for me!

In our large 18th century front window, to attract eyes of those walking by, I had placed a heated waterbed. That type of bed was unique in England and I was the first person to introduce it there, and later on the Continent, Africa, Middle East and the Far East. These were the systems that were so popular in the States in the late 60's, 70's and into the 80's. I had the bizarre idea that this type of bed, marketed for health and better sleep, might really catch on outside the States as well. So I invested my entire life's savings, all $17,000, and went into a new business, into countries with a product that was certainly unimaginable to the average person. Most people I knew thought that I was out of my mind.

The buzzer I had ordered to be put under the front door mat did its job, alerting me immediately that someone had come in. When I went into the front room to investigate, a rather well dressed though rain-damp gentleman stood, looking very seriously at the bed. I straightened my clothing and went to greet him, with perhaps somewhat of a forced smile. He quietly said hello and asked that I explain to him all I knew about the bed.

I could see he had not been drinking and his disposition was very somber. After I explained almost as much as I knew, he nodded earnestly and asked if the bed frame could be made of a different material than the wood one there, such as steel, and if the mattress could be deeper. Also, could the heating system be made to cool as well as heat and be reliable enough to hold a patient who was ill? The questions seemed to pour from his mouth, until I finally said, "Enough! Who are you, and what exactly are you looking for?"

The visitor looked embarrassed and apologized. He said, "I'm Dr. William Heald, Senior Surgeon at the major teaching hospital in England, Guy's Hospital. We have a severe problem and I believe this bed, with some changes, could be the answer. Not only for us, but perhaps for every hospital in and out of this country. Most hospitals have grave difficulties getting good trained nursing staff. That frequently results in decubitus ulcers, or bed sores. Not only are these painful, but they lengthen the time required for patients to stay in the hospital, escalating costs and taking up beds that other people need. We have one in our hospital, but it is many years old. It's very large, cannot be moved and needs to be filled with warm water every day, after we have drained out the cold water. We have no temperature control system at all. Yours is light years ahead."

I was mesmerized by Dr. Heald's words. I invited him to dinner. We went to a restaurant and stayed for hours. Then he basically concluded the evening with these words, "Last week we amputated the leg from an elderly man. We made perhaps the ultimate of mistakes and removed the wrong leg. To make a terrible error even worse, in days, he had pressure sores on many parts of his body. Many patients need to be turned every two hours, but we just don't have enough staff to do that. Please come to the hospital and see what we have and think of what you can do to help ameliorate this terrible problem." I actually had a feeling that much of my future destiny was spoken for. The next day I had a water bed delivered to Guy's Hospital.

I went to the hospital a few days later and met 82 year old Mr. Martin Free, who thanked me profusely for relieving him of so much pain. Then he said that he would be fine, and that it was much better that this happened to an older man like he was, than to a young person. No bitterness at all. Amazing!

As I was preparing to leave, I received a message to report to the hospital's board room. I wondered what I had gotten myself into, and quite concerned, entered a room with five people, all looking extremely serious.

"Please sit," said a very tall pin-striped suited man. "Sir," he began, "Your experimental bed is interesting and has obvious major advantages. However, you must make major changes if we and other institutions are to purchase them. Please make notes and get back to me as soon as possible." He then went into a litany of critical improvements health care institutions would require: the bodies must be made of steel or fiberglass not wood, as the organic matter retains odors. Plastic mattresses and liners should be furnished, which can be autoclaved and reused. Head and foot rests and safety side rails should be attached. Of course, the units should be on wheels that will make them mobile, so they can be moved into other rooms and wards. Requisite heights, weights and so on were detailed. I was aghast at so many requirements. Oh yes, epoxy, white color. I didn't even know what "epoxy white" meant! I wanted to shout, "Look, people, I'm in my 20's, and certainly without any finances to speak of." Instead, I spoke quietly and said that they were asking a great deal. If I could fulfill their requests, I would need to know some approximate purchasing figures. Mr.

Tall Pin-Striped looked at the others in the room and asked them to correct him if they disagreed. "Our hospital would want at least 20. More if the price is reasonable. If we can't afford to purchase all we want, then we'll rent them. But other hospitals in this and every other country should do the same. I would think you could be looking, in time, to orders in the thousands. But you will have to demonstrate them, lend them and work to make their value known."

Bells were going off and my thoughts were bursting with ideas. I just knew this was to be my future. How I would make it happen I had no idea, but make it happen I would. That's altogether another story. But the idea took root and grew. Within 18 months distributors came on board from very far indeed and I eventually moved from a London East End garage into major factories. Western Medical took shape. The beds were the best ever produced. The finest quality materials were always used and I made certain that the service was first rate. We sold over 5,000 bed units to hospitals eventually, in at least fifty countries. There was never a problem that occurred that we could not deal with easily. Additional thousands were rented, which was an added bonus. I was invited to join the BHEC, the British Health Care Council, their only member not born in England.

When I merged the company in 1985, and went on the London Stock Exchange, I felt I had done my best for myself and people requiring help in a great many hospitals around the world. In time, we even made a unit for the handicapped at home.

Eventually, there came a time for me to call it a day and I did so, moving to a quiet, very pleasurable life in Portugal. Sadly, two and a half years later the factories, the beds and the entire system I had spent so many years developing had been altered by greed. I was offered the opportunity to return as Chairman and restore it to its earlier luster. I declined with thanks. I never was comfortable going backwards.

GUY'S HOSPITAL, LONDON ... 1974

The following is an absurd, truthful story that is too ridiculous. Almost laughable, farcical, and painfully ludicrous. I don't believe one could just make this up. Quite to the contrary, it would have to be lived!

As I wrote in the preceding story, I had developed a unique bed system to treat patients who suffered from decubitus ulcers (bed sores), with the kind assistance of Professor William Heald, Senior Surgeon at Guy's Hospital. This particular day I was paying a social and hopefully intellectual visit to that outstanding old teaching hospital.

I clearly recall the very cold day it had turned into. I was wearing a heavy suit, waistcoat or vest, shirt and tie, all enclosed in a black and white tweed overcoat. Quite warm, but elegant. Hours later I was to regret that.

The professor and I were, for some reason, in a small, cramped room that held various items required by the staff: cabinets full of medicines, and just behind where I was standing, scissors, syringes, many glass items, and so forth, all held in glass bowls, resting in specific places on metal carts. Professor Heald was showing me photographs of a patient we were to visit, and I reached out to see one a bit clearer. That's when he noted I had a ganglion on my wrist. For anyone not aware, that's a fairly large, clearly raised sore. He said that it really should be removed and it wouldn't take him more than a few minutes to "slice" it off. I was paying little attention to it, and said he should do whatever he wanted.

Now, remember, I'm in a very well heated small room, wearing an overcoat and dressed very warmly. Dr. Heald and I were speaking and looking at these photos and we were standing the entire time. He commented that he should get some bandages, as there would be blood and fluid shortly coming from the area he was cutting. It was only then that I looked down and saw this mess flowing out from my wrist. He berated himself and said that these were not the ideal circumstances to do this operation, noting that I was starting to perspire. Then I recall him asking if I was all right. Of course I said yes. This was just a few seconds before I realized the room was moving all around me.

The next thing I remember is loud, critical voices, and me laying on the floor. Apparently, Dr. Heald had hit a vein with the scalpel. That set off various vibrations in my brain and I fell over … backwards, hitting the back of my head with the tray that held all the glass and instruments. That made for quite a bit of glass going into the back my scalp. I sat up, saw three or four nurses and began apologizing profusely. This fell on deaf ears as the professor was now continuously apologizing as well. He said that he should have had me sitting, not standing up, and that all my heavy clothing should have been removed. This mutual apologetic charade continued, until one of the staff stated that she felt she had removed all the glass in my head. However, I should certainly get an x-ray, to be certain I did not have a severe concussion.

My objections were ignored and I was taken down to the first floor where the x-ray equipment was. There were quite a few people there waiting their turn. I told the person to leave me, as I was fine and would wait in my place in line. He left, and I just went to sleep. Totally unconscious. At least twenty other people went in before me. Finally, I was tapped on the shoulder and asked why I had not gone into the x-ray room when called. I was then taken into this large room, perhaps 100 years old or more, and told to lie on a table. I was still completely dressed. As I surveyed the walls, I noted that all were in desperate need of a coat of paint. They had sandbags that were tied to the heavy x-ray machines, making them easier to raise and lower to the patient. I wondered how old this mechanism was. It seemed practically archaic to me. Almost from a different century, long past. Then I blinked as I saw the sandbag being used to lower the equipment for me suddenly break loose from its moorings. It took only a few seconds, but I vividly remember the missile gliding straight for my head! It was spot on target. It weighed about 50 pounds, and was probably more than three feet long. I never stood a chance of avoiding it. The collision with my now screaming head was deafening, and I was blown off the table. The orderly helped me up and I believe was trying to apologize as he placed me back on the table. This time they were able to take x-rays.

For some foolish reason, I thought I needed to see the professor before I left. Somehow I found the elevators and was the last person to get into the one that appeared. Meaning, I would be the first person off. When we arrived at the main floor, I took one step and something immediately ripped into my shins; it was someone pushing a metal wheelchair, obviously in a hurry. I don't know if I cried before I hit the floor or afterwards. However, it felt as if both of my legs had exploded. I'm pleased to say the person pushing the wheelchair realized he was moving too fast and instantly apologized. So it was my wrist, head, head again, and now my shins. When I opened my eyes, Jimmy O'Sullivan, one of my delivery men, was there. Also the professor and a host of others, all wanting to know why this well dressed man was sprawled out on the floor! I can say with authority that I have never been apologized to more frequently, in such a short period of time, than in that hospital visit.

Jimmy asked if I had had a heart attack. Looking up, I calmly replied, "Not yet, but perhaps soon." I was helped to my feet and the fellow from the x-ray department appeared. He then told of the fiasco that took place downstairs. Professor Heald spoke of the disaster that had taken place with the scalpel, and the orderly spoke of his urgency with the wheelchair. I have never seen a professional staff so frozen in their places. Jimmy tried to make light of it and said it was a good thing that I was in a hospital. I could only stare at him and say, "Oh, quite right, James. Now if it isn't too difficult, would you kindly take me elsewhere. It doesn't matter where. My office, my home, anywhere. But please take me away."

When the day started, it was a beautiful, sunshine-filled day. Now it was pouring rain. I discovered that I had left my umbrella inside. But no way was I ever going to go back inside Guy's Hospital again. I haven't to this day.

A SPECIAL RESTAURANT

I was staying a few months a year in Bangkok, Thailand, a week at a time. Because of the large size of the medical equipment I was shipping, I decided it would be prudent to build a factory there. Thus, with a Chinese partner, whom I was obligated to take, I was now in business in the Far East.

It was easy to enjoy the Thai people and the country, and as an employer I found it easy also to be very kind to my staff. In turn, they made no secret of the fact that they appreciated my way of doing business.

During this period, I remember distinctly a remarkable thing that happened. It was a national holiday. I was invited to lunch along with three of the guys from the factory, and accepted without a second thought. Our hosts met us at a boat dock and we boarded a small canoe-like vessel. The boatman moved us downriver.

Unfortunately, we had to carry weapons, but we were lucky and they were not needed on this voyage.

As we glided along in the water that day that I saw a peculiar fish head rise above the surface, with a straight body following its head. The creature looked somewhat like the descriptions of Scotland's legendary Loch Ness Monster. I called it a "fish-snake." We finally reached the so-called restaurant, in reality a small wooden shell. To get into the place you needed to climb out of the boat, meaning soak yourselves from the knees down. We climbed up and were met by people who were very helpful; they gave us new temporary shoes to put on. The place was immaculately clean but smelled of fish the moment you entered. Not a salubrious place by any means, I thought.

The restaurant owner led us into a back room filled with huge makeshift fish tanks. There were all kinds of fish and shellfish, and as I gazed at them, one of those heads rose up, like the fish I had seen from the boat. I was completely awe-struck.

There is no possible way that I can adequately describe the flavors I enjoyed during that meal. A variety of the fish were steamed, grilled, or roasted. Never before and never since that time have I tasted and appreciated a meal as much as I did that one. So simple, yet so exotic. And if you're wondering, yes, I did go back and was treated as well as I had been originally. I was again served lots of that odd mixture of fish, but never have I had a meal as superb as that first one. In the middle of nowhere.

BEIRUT ... 1977

As the proud owner of Western Medical, now with three factories and distributors throughout Europe, the Far East and Middle East, I usually traveled from my home in London 10 out of 30 days a month. My journeys would take me to different places to stimulate sales and meet with clients. On the day of this story, I was in Beirut, which is often called "Little Paris," its namesake being my favorite city. This happened to be a good last day of the month for me, because I had concluded my business early and had a comfortable amount of time to myself. I could simply walk along the beach road, passing by the many lovely hotels and restaurants. Although there was some civil unrest in Lebanon, it rarely came into this charming city.

My adventure began at midday. It was sunny, but not too warm and frankly I was feeling quite good about life itself. That was about to change. As I crossed the street intending to go to one of the cafés for a glass of wine, a car with three men pulled alongside me. "Nice to see you back here," one of the passengers said. I simply smiled and replied that the pleasure was mine. Suddenly the two passenger side doors opened and two young men got out. They were now not smiling. "Get in, Nigel." I backed away and said my name was not Nigel and that I had no intention of joining them. A short mustachioed fellow pointed downwards and that was when I saw he was holding a pistol. I tried to say something but the men became very agitated and grabbed my jacket. Within seconds I was in the back seat and we were speeding away. I was in good shape and still sparred twice a week at my gym on Wigmore Street, in London's West End. But common sense was the better part of valor and I just tried to make light of whatever it was that they wanted.

I was surprised that we were not taking some little drive but in fact were heading up a craggy mountain. During our trip, the men spoke on occasion to each other, but not a word in English. When I tired to say something, all I received were dirty looks. Almost two hours after we started I saw a sign in English that said "Baalbek." I was familiar with the name as a place which had a marvelous theater in the round, where concerts were frequently held.

When we reached a very rocky hill, I was told to get out. The men followed and I was ordered with a wave of the pistol to start climbing. One of the men drove off and the other two started climbing alongside me. No grass or trees, just dirt and endless stones and rocks. Halfway up one of them slipped and I automatically grabbed him, perhaps preventing him from being injured seriously. We stopped to catch our breath, and the men smiled for the first time at me. When we completed the climb we were in a very large clearing sprinkled with some rather pleasant small houses. I then saw some women and a few children. I was totally confused.

I was taken to wash up and then a boy about 10 years old, in his best English, told me to rest up and we would eat shortly. Any thoughts of my being killed were gone, as they would have done that earlier. My only assumption was that I was being kidnapped for money. I assumed they never bound me simply because where was I going to run to? Why they had decided to take me up the mountain, I never could figure out.

For three days I lived with my kidnappers, being treated adequately, which I later learned was because I prevented the one from falling. When I asked the boy why I was being held a prisoner, he looked perplexed and said, "The money." I thought that there were certainly better targets for a kidnapping than me, and just could not figure it out. The boy then said the big boss was coming tomorrow and I better have the money. So at least this ordeal was finally going to come to a conclusion shortly. One way or another.

The next day the boy called me to stand by him for his interpretation. I heard the sound of cars and was very surprised to see a perfectly clear road behind one of the houses. Two very dusty but new cars pulled up to us. The three men who had originally grabbed me were in one and four others were in the other car.

From the back seat a very sinister looking, heavyset man emerged: long hair, big stomach, a pistol in his belt, with very deep-set eyes. He glared at me and looked angrier by the second. There were harsh words between him and the first three men. He then came right to my face and said in excellent English, "Sorry, but my men have made a mistake. I had advanced hashish to a fellow named Nigel and he was supposed to come back and pay me. He never has. They will take you back to Beirut." I gave him a look and said, "That's not good enough. My clothes are ruined and I missed my flight back to England. I think you should pay these costs." Immediately after I said it, I realized how idiotic that must have sounded. Then, for the first time, he smiled and said that I was right! The mistake was theirs. He went to his car and removed a briefcase, opened it and handed me ten one hundred dollar bills. As I had already proved that I was bordering on insanity, I held my hand out for more! He gave me five more and said that he felt that was quite enough. I then smiled and said I agreed. I had actually made a profit!

Before they took me back, we sat and had a meal with a drink called Arak that almost burned a hole in my stomach. When they offered me hashish I could only laugh and decline with thanks.

On the flight home I smiled all the way. I had not been physically harmed and had had a fascinating experience. Plus, previously I was holding a Coach Class ticket. Now I was able to buy one in First Class!

MOSCOW 1978 ... MY FIRST VISIT

I have no idea why I was told my room was in the Hotel Leningradsky. I had never heard of the place, but Intourist Services had arranged everything. From the airport, I had exited onto the front steps to find a taxi driver holding up a cardboard sign with my name on it. As I was getting into his vehicle, he seemed no more pleased to see me than I was to see him. He placed my suitcase in the car. This was an era when many men carried their special belongings in what was somewhat of a masculine handbag. My handbag was secured tightly around my left wrist.

Arriving at the hotel, I checked in at the massive front desk, only to discover I was already registered. I asked to see the room before I gave my credit card and was extremely pleased to see that it was in fact a suite, but charged as a regular room. Later I learned it had been reserved for a prominent speaker with a similar name. Although aging, the hotel was being kept up in fine condition. The restaurant was lavish … but the food, diabolical. Basically there was nothing I could or would eat there.

This was a Medical symposium and supposedly one of the most important held in Russia. The days ran into nights and I was totally bored. That first evening as I took one of the tired lifts to my floor, a lovely girl joined me. Musky in color, she nevertheless was marvelous to my eyes. My first thought was that she was, shall I say, a "lady of the night." Wrong. She was the daughter of an ambassador who was stationed there. There were older women on every floor making notes, especially of who went into which rooms. But we laughed and she was my guest. In my refrigerator there was vodka and caviar, compliments of the hotel, or a previous guest. We drank and spoke and enjoyed each other's company. Later, in bed, she touched my shoulder and pointed out a camera in the ceiling. I spoke to the camera, telling whoever was viewing us that I would appreciate a copy of the tape. Oh, they could keep the original, but this was a wonderful memory and a film would be a delightful keepsake. About five minutes later, we noticed that the red light had turned off.

The next day when I asked at the desk to purchase a copy of the film, all I received were blank stares. Of course no one knew anything about a camera or a film. When I re-entered my suite, there was no longer a camera. No surprise.

The next night four male associates and I decided to go out to a highly recommended club and restaurant. The food was no better than that at the hotel, and the jugglers, bicycle riders and belly dancers were a bit difficult to watch, but we did our best to be polite. About midnight we decided we'd had enough. For some reason we never learned, each of us was staying in a different hotel. It's not that way today, but then, it was. I'm by nature somewhat suspicious of new people around me. When we left, I placed each guy in a different taxi, with me planning to be in the last. I was tired but relaxed; it seemed as if it was just going to be another boy's evening out. A black sedan pulled up, but I couldn't tell if it was a taxi or not. The doorman seemed to edge me inside. I was reluctant as I saw people occupying it. However, I was very tired and the driver asked which hotel, so I told him and simply went along. That was a bad move. To my left was a very large man, and an equally big lady was on my right. There was a mountain of a man in the front seat and the driver had an unpleasant sneer on his face.

I said in a loud voice, "This isn't necessary. Take my bag, there is money in it, and just take me to the Hotel Leningradsky." The huge man in front turned and said, "Oh, friend, relax, we are going to a party!" I could only think of Beirut and smile. We drove in quite a circle. My guess is that we covered in half an hour that which could have been done in fifteen minutes maximum. I knew it wasn't a robbery as I had offered my bag. A kidnapping? Doubtful that they would go to that extent. OK, I thought, just stay awake and deal with this as best possible. The only humorous thing was that these people were so large, that if I tried I could easily outrun them. It crossed my mind but I dismissed it.

Finally in the darkness — no street lamps were on — we pulled up to a large apartment complex. They led me to a fire escape which I understood I was to climb. There were always two of these giants around me, so I felt it was much easier to play their game. The driver of the taxi looked at me and said, "My name is Boris. Not to worry, this is just a party."

We climbed up three flights of very cold steel steps. Boris moved in front and with his fist, knocked on the door in a special rhythm. I obviously had no idea what to expect. It was then I decided I wouldn't go inside without a fight.

The steel door opened, and I heard that voice: "You ain't nothing but a hound dog, crying all the time." Elvis Presley? Big Boris came to me and said, "I told you it was a party." When I walked in I saw vodka, water, caviar and all sorts of foods. I was told to relax, drink, eat, and to let him know if there was a particular girl there I fancied. Well, those ladies could play for the Green Bay Packers! No, I was certainly not interested. But I would smile and play the game. These people weren't thieves or even villains. Boris brought over that day's copy of the *Financial Times*. He said that they would APPRECIATE it if we could exchange currencies. They would add even more rubles to my return, so in fact I would have a profit! Like I really wanted rubles! I had a number of different currencies with me, Dutch, British, French, German, American, about $100 dollars each, so that I would be covered if I was in those countries and needed a taxi. Not a fortune. But I saw in their eyes they truly needed foreign money, and this was plenty. I said I wanted no profit, but that I should have some of that money when I go back to the hotel, to prove I was not robbed. We agreed easily on about half and they were very pleased. It was now about 3:00 a.m. and we were all tired. They left a woman with me, who realized all I wanted was to return to my hotel. She showed me the way out. Shortly later I climbed down the fire escape and started walking to my lodgings, having no clue where I was. The few street cleaners I met spoke no English, so I just kept looking up for lights. It was at least an hour later when I saw a familiar landmark. Eventually, about 5:30 a.m., I made it to the hotel. But there I was met by two very upset KGB men. They were supposed to keep an eye on all of us and I had disappeared. I acted very angry, and told them that two bearded men had kidnapped me, but became drunk and I escaped. In reality, none of the men I was with had a beard. They were just trying to make a better life for themselves and their families. There was no reason to describe them. The two KBG fellows and I went up to my room, and as they had waited all night in the lobby looking for me, they were hungry and thirsty. They finished all my vodka and caviar and went to sleep. I showered and went to my meetings. It had been a very long interesting evening.

SOUTH AFRICA ... 1979

I was in my office in London when I welcomed John Theron from Cape Town, South Africa. We had an appointment and he was spot on time. He was a young man in his late 30's, large, about 6'5", and approaching 300 pounds. Nevertheless, he moved sleekly, not as a huge person. He had a big face with a marvelous smile. My first impression was that he was comfortable to be around.

We spent hours together, learning about each other, as well as heightening his knowledge of my medical equipment. When I picked up the dinner bill, I knew I would rather dress him than feed him. He did place an impressive first order for equipment before he left, and we agreed on many subjects that included much of South Africa. He was an educated lawyer and not without funds or contacts. My knowledge of his region of the world was limited. I appreciated hearing firsthand as much as I could of it. To my surprise he quickly became one of my finest and largest clients.

About a year later he invited me to visit the first medical exhibition ever held there. England and South Africa are great allies, thus no problems in that regard. I would fly there and he insisted I stay at his home with his wife and children. He had a large house above the bay, in a wonderful location. I flew South African Airways, to help get a feel of my destination. It proved to be a poor decision, as something went wrong in the cockpit and we had to make an emergency landing in Zambia. About 7:00 a.m. we were awakened from a restless night's sleep. The pilot calmly explained our predicament, and said that if they did not have the needed part there, one would be flown in, in a few short hours. In the meantime, we could stretch our legs, have breakfast and shortly be on our way. The man was either a dreamer or naïve.

We landed at a wooden airport that looked incredibly ominous. But the pilots managed the runway with great panache and skill, and we landed with no difficulties. Yet.

After a long meeting with the airport staff, we were told that passengers holding South African passports had to remain on the plane. Others could get off. That created a problem. We were not about to get off separated from the entire group. The toilets were backed up. There was no food or water on the plane and many passengers were getting upset. A sort of terrible deal was worked out that left no doubt but that S.A. Airways was being taken for a nasty ride. After an hour or so we were all allowed to get off and go into the so-called terminal. All they were prepared to serve was stale bread and warm beer. No water. Prices were many times higher than usual. Not one single person bought a thing. After a few hours they warmed the bread. Still no one moved. I was craving water. However, no one even made a request. I followed their lead. Then seven soldiers bearing weapons arrived. As I started to become alarmed, a man we called John Wayne arrived from South Africa. He was a massive man, and came with not only the spare part, but with another fully refreshed airplane! The Zambians were not happy, but we were thrilled!

We took off and landed in Johannesburg, where I caught a connection to Cape Town and another true adventure. John and a friend, another lawyer, had been waiting hours to meet me. I expect I looked like an escaped convict. Unshaven, clothes wrinkled and probably smelling bad. What a great example of a chairman of a growing medical company! But they were wearing bathing suits and T-shirts. I was a bit confused, especially when I heard we were going fishing. Off came my jacket and tie, and happily I put on the clothing they lent me. I still had my suitcase in the car but had no idea where we were going. Simply put, we were about to break the law. It's called poaching! They passed a bottle of fine whiskey around that I was certain would kill me, although in hindsight, I suppose it likely relaxed any fears I had. Off in John's Jeep we raced to the secret watering hole. Driving with two lawyers, I assumed I was in safe hands.

Wearing just goggles and a bathing suit, John drove to the light blue lagoon. Harry, the other lawyer and I stood on the grass knoll above him. I watched in some horror as John vanished deep into the water, and the pool turned crimson red. The lobsters were not giving up without a fight. They dug their claws into any part of him they could. He was being systematically torn. Whenever he re-emerged, it was always with live lobsters chewing away at him. Suddenly Harry went into action. He grabbed what looked like an old sack, but it was really lined, tough fabric. He went close to the water's edge and Big John started hurling the lobsters into the sack. They were clawing away at him in a frenzy to get loose. None escaped as one after the other was thrown into the sack. He still wasn't finished as Harry brought out yet another special bag. His aim was incredibly true and more lobsters flew through the air, adding further bounty to what we already had collected. John looked at me and yelled, "I know you don't eat meat, and when I was with you in London you picked up all the bills. Well, now it's time for me to pay you back. These are the best lobsters in the world, mate, and you will have them for breakfast, lunch and dinner! Grilled, fried, sautéed, baked, you name it. We South Africans always pay our debts! Enjoy!"

When we returned to his wonderful home, his wife came out to meet us. We were alive, healthy and not under arrest. The wine flowed and we exchanged stories and lots of lies.

One day on what turned out to be my first of several visits with John and his family, I walked to the post office to send cards. I was shocked to see two lines, one labeled "Europeans," the other ... "Coloreds." There was a wooden wall separating the races. On my second visit two years later, the sign was still up. But the timber wall was down and only a rope divided us. I went back two years later for the last time. Both the rope and the signs had vanished. We were now standing shoulder to shoulder, smiling and shaking hands. Not overnight, but it did finally happen.

One day after this last visit, I received a call in London from John, saying that his brother's farm, in what was then known as Rhodesia, now Zimbabwe, was under attack. John, family and friends decided to go there and help as much as possible. Sadly, more sadly than I can say, I never heard from them again.

May they rest in peace.

INTERESTING TIMES IN CAIRO, EGYPT 1970 – 1984

The British Hospital Export Council (BHEC) joined with like bodies from a number of other countries to hold a joint Medical exhibition in Cairo. As a member of the British Council, I immediately decided to attend. The venue selected was a very basic one, but it seemed no one knew how to deal with the building's facilities. To make matters worse, when our meetings took place, the temperatures in Cairo were running a steamy 90 - 100 degrees. Electricity and water were last minute thoughts. If exhibitors and visitors did not bring water bottles from the hotel, there wasn't a drop available. An enterprising youngster about 14 years old approached everyone quietly and offered to sell bottled water for about the same price as the hotels did. Almost all attendees agreed. No one wanted to be ill from unclean water.

When the doors opened, letting guests in, I met an interesting guy who owned his own medical equipment company. This was somewhat unique, as before this time, the state purchased all equipment for hospitals. Dealing with them was no pleasure and in most cases companies just decided not to. He and I were having a pleasant conversation when the young water boy came by for our next order. I told him another few bottles and off he went. Everyone thought that his father or friend had a quantity of plastic bottles on a truck out in the back. The gentleman I was speaking with smiled and asked me to follow him. We went outside and I saw the boy filling bottles from the building's tap water, which was almost a guarantee of having cramps in the morning. Although I cancelled our orders and advised many others what they were drinking, some still went ahead and ordered more.

My new acquaintance was named Dr. Adel El Kady. A pleasant, inquisitive and personable fellow. He explained his family had helped raise funds for him to start his own company, but by no means was he wealthy. I respected his honesty and agreed to meet him for dinner at the Sheraton later that evening. After a short time I lowered my minimum order so that he could purchase what he could afford and we were in business. After some three or four years his company grew and it was always nice to revisit him.

One night he was late for dinner and when he did show, he explained that he had been called at the last minute to deliver a baby. As the husband was a high ranking politician, Adel had to agree. I've no idea why, but instead of canceling the evening's dinner, I offered to join him at the hospital. The birth was not an easy one and he asked for my opinion, as if I had a clue what to do. I simply said he was doing fine and to carry on. It was a short time later that a son was born and the parents were thrilled. As it was their first, they named him Adel, after the doctor, and Ali, which is the name I used in the Arab Middle East.

This was the second boy who was given a name of mine. As I wrote in a story about the time I was living in Brussels, the first baby boy named for me was born in Israel while I was visiting. So now I have an Ali and an Alon, who might be shooting at each other one day.

The day after "our" delivery, Adel invited me to a local restaurant that he enjoyed often. The owner was a long time friend, Ibrahim. The meal was primarily vegetarian, so I was more than pleased. The good doctor thanked me for my help at the hospital, which made it difficult for me to keep a straight face. Then his belt beeper rang, he looked at the number, excused himself, and asked to use the telephone at the desk. As I watched him I could see that there was a problem. He came to the table and asked to be pardoned for cutting the evening short, but it was his brother Atef advising him that their Father was very ill. I offered to take a taxi back to my hotel. However, he insisted and took me back himself.

Later the next afternoon, the expo ended and my group was packing things up when I saw Adel walking to me. His father had passed away, but it was expected as he had smoked continuously everyday throughout his life. Then came the surprise that left me speechless. Adel invited me to be one of the honored pallbearers carrying the coffin to the place of their religious service, and then down the street where a hearse would take the immediate family to his grave. I had dined with Adel, Atef and the father on a few occasions, always waving the cigarette smoke away, which gave the older man a good laugh. Our conversations covered a diverse array of subjects and often lasted long into the night. At any rate, I immediately agreed and times and places were arranged.

The next day a driver collected me and we drove silently to the mosque. They gave me some garments to put on and I was escorted to the seat I was to occupy. An odd feeling came over me and I looked around. It was Atef's eyes staring insolently at me. I knew they were aware that I was not a Muslim and perhaps not even a Christian. Religion was a subject that was one of the few I never raised. But they understood that I was not there to do any harm to anyone. Quite the opposite, I only brought health care and relief of pain. Perhaps it was a jealousy of his better educated and respected brother Adel, but there was no love between the two of them. Adel had tried many times to show Atef he cared. Always he was rebuffed. As for me, I was still in awe that I had been asked, and helped to lift the coffin and walk it down the streets of Cairo. I felt no fear, only a sadness for the body resting inside.

Over the next few years I visited Egypt often and Adel even came to London where we enjoyed many wonderful hours together. His business was doing very well and I went out of my way to show him as much of my personal London as possible. He was delighted.

It was a few months later when I was actually preparing the itinerary for my next trip to the Middle East, which would obviously include Cairo, when a call came through from Adel's secretary. Atef wanted me to know that Adel was killed in an auto accident. Now that the company was completely his, Atef had decided to sell it to the Government. There was no reason for me to stop by their office, which would soon be closed. I tried to speak with her to find out when, where and other details, but she said that Atef had told her to say just what she had and not another word. I understood and it crossed my mind that he could have been standing next to her, monitoring the call. All I then said was that my heart was with the family and that I hoped to see them soon to offer my condolences in person. She only said, "Shokran," thank you in Arabic, and we were disconnected.

When I was next in Cairo I walked in the general direction of the restaurant where Adel had been so comfortable. I recalled it was next to a bridge, and in a short time I found it. I saw Ibrahim standing outside fixing a large umbrella over a table. I was pleased that he recognized me. We shook hands and I ordered a light meal. When I was finished he sent me a glass of Arak. A strong clear drink, not unlike the Greek Ouzo. I invited him to sit and have one with me. There was a sad silence. "You know about Adel, yes"? I nodded my head and said his secretary called and said there was a car accident. He only sneered and then asked if I was familiar with the different bibles. "Not all, but some," I said. I could see the veins in his neck start to stand out. He then whispered, "Do you remember the part about the two brothers?" I hesitated, not wanting to say the wrong thing. "Cain and Able?" Ibrahim nodded affirmatively. "We never even saw the body to bury him. Atef had taken care of everything. "Ibrahim spit on his own sidewalk." Adel liked you very much, and often spoke of you," he said. "Atef … well he is a different person."

The next day I went to the government office, which now dealt with my products. During the conversation with these new people I mentioned my sorrow over Adel's passing. One faceless man said, "Yes, that was bad, and his brother Atef also died in a car accident just last night, too bad. Although I have heard he was not very obliging when it came to our negotiations." Then a bit of a smile. "But the family will still be paid in full. Inshallah. Please God." I knew that would never happen. "Now," the man said, "Let's get down to business." I could only cringe inside. My mouth was dry and I asked for the men's room. He reluctantly pointed out where to go. I went through the doors and kept on walking, never to return to the table. All business in the future was done by telex and letters. My homage and respect to an old friend.

The Man Now

And The Man Then

Age 19

1940's
Mom with
Brother Steve
and me, in front
of our home in
Philadelphia

Dad with Brother
Steve and me
at the beach,
Sea Isle, N.J.

The first a.k.a. -- Rocky Mintziano

Top, center: playing half-back for Miami Beach High School. He went on to play halfback and outside line-backer for the University of Miami, under coach Andy Gustafson. Below, Left: "Rocky Mintziano during workout.

Meeting Boxing Heroes

Top, Muhammad Ali, with Rocky and others from the world of sports and media. Right a pair of Rocky's gloves. Below, Rocky, (L) Joe Bogner, World Heavyweight Champ, Samuel Montague, a wealthy aristocrat

Alon a.k.a. Adam Savage

"I don't even play the piano."

NAKED CITY

3 Shows

Adam Savage with British star Jack Hawkins

And now, Introducing The Serial Entrepreneur

LOS ANGELES EVENING AND SUNDAY
HERALD EXAMINER
CLASSIFIED ADVERTISING

RICK MILES — Richmond 8-4111

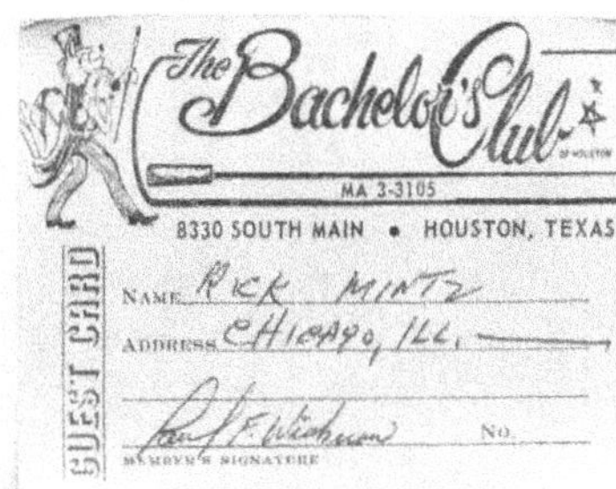
The Bachelor's Club of Houston
MA 3-3105
8330 SOUTH MAIN • HOUSTON, TEXAS
GUEST CARD
NAME RICK MINTZ
ADDRESS CHICAGO, ILL.
MEMBER'S SIGNATURE
No.

MANUFACTURERS OF SPECIALIZED MEDICAL EQUIPMENT
WESTERN MEDICAL GROUP

A. MINTZ
CHAIRMAN C. E. O.

WESTERN MEDICAL CENTRE.
26 NEW CAVENDISH STREET, LONDON. W1N 7LH.
TELEPHONE: 01-935. 7209/7210/6145
TELEX: 912882 COMNET G ID: WES

ALAN MINTZ, District Sales Representative
6610 Iris Street
Hollywood, California
Telephone: 465-1451

DYMO

DYMO INDUSTRIES, INC.
Box 1030 Berkeley 1, California
Telephone 654-7272 Area Code 415

COMMONWEALTH OF PENNSYLVANIA
DEPARTMENT OF BANKING
PENNSYLVANIA SECURITIES COMMISSION
No. 7264
The Commission Neither Recommends Nor Assumes Responsibility For Securities Offered By The Dealer or Salesman
ALAN MINTZ
4944 WYNNEFIELD AVE., PHILA., PA.
This certifies that the salesman named above has been registered ... provisions of "The Pennsylvania Securities Act" approved the ... July, 1941, as a SALESMAN of the duly registered dealer named ... registration expires March ...
JANOV & CO., PHILA., PA.
IN TESTIMONY WHEREOF, The Pennsylvania Securities Commission has caused these presents to be signed and authenticated by its ... attested by the Secretary at its office in the City of Harrisburg, this
26th day of June 1961
Attest: Secretary
Revised PSCF-5—12M—1-60
Commissioners
1961

MICHIGAN 2-0800

ALAN MINTZ

SPECIAL REPRESENTATIVE
THE SEEBURG SALES CORPORATION
1500 N. DAYTON STREET — CHICAGO 22

FORTY-TWO PRODUCTS, LTD., INC.
EXECUTIVE TOILETRIES LTD.

RICK MINTZ

OFFICES AND LABORATORIES — RESIDENCE: 465-1451
1649 - 19TH STREET, SANTA MONICA, CALIF. - GR 7-4242 - UP 0-0242

BEKINS
ARCHIVAL SERVICES

ALAN R. MINTZ

190 OTIS STREET
SAN FRANCISCO, CALIF. 94103
TELEPHONE 621-3520

BUSINESS RECORDS CENTERS • BEKINS FILM CENTERS

Western Waterbeds

Western Waterbeds -- Foundation of an International Medical Equipment Business

Founded by Alon in London, in the sixties, Western Waterbeds morphed almost immediately into a manufacturer providing waterbeds specially designed for medical purposes. The company expanded to a number of countries and in time acquired related medical product manufacturing facilities, such as the ones featured on pages following.

Low pressure fluid support systems for prevention & healing of pressure sores

Alon/Ali's Western Medical Groups has been credited with helping thousands of people recover from a variety of health problems worldwide.

Scott-Western

Bedpan and urine bottle washer/disinfector

Model SW90

WESTERN MEDICAL LIMITED

26 NEW CAVENDISH STREET, LONDON W1M 7LH

TEL: 01-935 7209/7210/8145 TELEX: AMSTELCO 21879 ATT: WESTMED

P R E S S   R E L E A S E

The Western Medical Group of Companies has acquired the entire engineering plant and assets of an old and established company, Westbourne Industrial Engineering, Ltd., in Poole, Dorset, England. All of the present staff are being retained.

The newly acquired company will manufacture steel products and equipment used in the health-care industry.

With a growing range of products, increased export growth, and a solid order book, The Group is expanding its' capacity for self-reliance.

Above, early press release announces Western Medical's acquisition of Westbourne Industrial Engineering, Ltd., in Dorset, which gave Alon and his staff expanded capabilities in manufacture and design. Right, Alon supervises loading of Western Waterbed van in the early days, with original notes about the photo.

Alon Mintz, President of Western Waterbeds, is seen here supervising the loading of his most unusual pick up truck - a double decker London bus - converted to be the travelling sales and show-room for the highly popular waterbed.
Air Canada flies the consignments direct from the USA and Air Canada's Cargo Sales Representative Bob Williamson, who has masterminded the air lift of beds from Western USA, is seen top right of the picture.

As is his wont, Alon greatly enjoyed creating this business, and in the course of developing products was delighted to meet fascinating and distinguished individuals around the globe.

Above, in the Philippines, Imelda Marcos (far right), with nurses, listens to Alon. Pictured below, from left, Minister of Economics, Paris Embassy, Alon, First Commercial Secretary, Paris Embassy, Frank Harris, British Health-Care Export Council,

SALON MONDIAL DE REANIMATION PARIS 1977 **Photo by Paul Foucha**

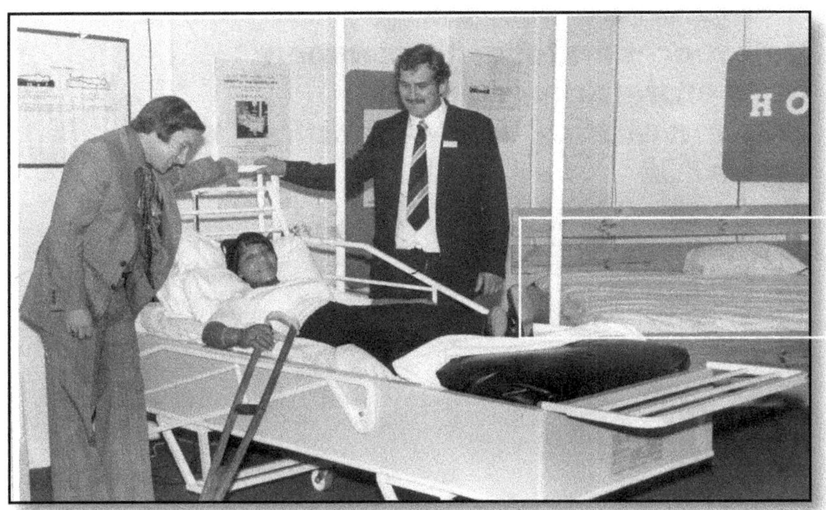

Above, Alon and John Theron demonstrate the healing properties of Western Medical beds with nurse at expo in Capetown, South Africa. Below, Alon discusses Western Medical waterbed with Princess Margaret of Great Britain.

References and specific comments from professional users of Western Medical Water Flotation Units Series 800

Extract of a report from Dr C I Gryfe, Medical Director, Baycrest Centre for Geriatric Care, Toronto, Canada, and Dr R H Fisher, Head of Extended Care Department, Sunnybrook Medical Centre, Toronto, Canada.

"Effective avoidance of pressure was achieved by using the principle of flotation in the treatment of 4 particularly refractory cases who had been under our continuous care for at least 3 months with decubitus ulcers.

Conclusion: "The Western Medical Water Flotation Unit appears to be an effective and practicable means of rapidly treating refractory bedsores."

Guy's Hospital, London, England; (R J Heald FRCS Senior Surgical Registrar)

"The saving of nursing time can be immense, and the advantages for the patient who must be nursed at home are obvious."

If traction is necessary for a fracture the counter-traction provided by the large area of contact is excellent. I personally believe that the time will come when every ward has a few of these Waterbeds for people who are in special danger of developing bed sores."

Greenwich District Hospital, London, England (Extract of letter from Dr Gorst).

"A female 90-year-old CVA patient became virtually bedbound, requiring full-time nursing care and not moving at all of her own accord. By using a Western Medical waterbed a deep infected bedsore of long standing which was deteriorating rapidly had its down-wards course abruptly reversed and began to heal visibly for the first time in 8 months. The bed presented no problems in use and the nurses reported that the patient seemed very much more comfortable and relaxed than when on a conventional mattress or a ripple bed."

Middleburg Hospital, Germany (Dr Paulsen, Head Physician).

"With the help of a water flotation bed an old woman with 2 decubitus ulcers was healed within a three week period. The short healing process is unusual and therefore remarkable. This device offers a considerable assistance to the nurse and subjective comfort for the patient."

Neumann-Heim Hospital, Hamburg, Germany (Dr M Fritsch, Chief Physician).

"Savings of 60% of working hours can be achieved with the use of this water flotation unit for immobilized patients, or those seriously ill, because the nursing requirements are considerably reduced. The duration of the in-patient treatment needed for a pressure sore becomes much shorter because of the rapid healing process. The costs of treatment (operations, expensive drugs) are greatly reduced.

"Geriatric Nursing" – Nurses Aid Series (published by Bailliere Tindall) 1981 "Pressure Sores and their Prevention" A. M. F. Storrs, S.R.N., S.C.N.

"The water bed has eased the nurse's burden of preventing and treating pressure sores successfully. Fluid flotation therapy reduces the pressure on susceptible parts of the body, thus preventing, as well as curing pressure sores. Western Medical have developed the water bed system throughout the world and have proved that not only is continuous pressure reduction achieved, so that the patient can remain in a static position, and be moved less frequently, if necessary, but also skin friction and irritation are reduced. Temperature control prevents perspiration and the use of these units can save considerable costs of patient treatment.

Extract of Report by Dr Ryan, Freeman Hospital, Newcastle on Tyne, England

"The Relevance of Low-pressure Patient Support Systems for Intensive Therapy"

It is generally agreed that three support systems prevent and cure decubitus ulcers. These are as follows in increasing order of cost:

1. Water flotation bed (Western Medical type)
2. 'Low air-loss' bed (Mediscus type)
3. Fluidised silica bead bed (Clinitron)

St Elisabeth Hospital, Antwerp, Belgium (Dr R Kaivers, Chief Physician)

"A spastic, immobilised patient with flexural contractures of both arms and legs developed multiple bed sores, in spite of intensive care. Because of the contorted position of this patient, the treatment of these bed sores was a difficult problem. When using a water flotation bed, without changing the specific or general treatment procedure, the bed sores started to heal. Because of an interruption in the use of the waterbed, the patient had to be placed in a normal bed for one day. This caused part of the new tissue granulation to start to break down. One week later on the waterbed, this breakdown was healed."

St Georges Hospital, Hamburg, Germany (Dr Treu)

"This bed represents a very effective improvement in the prophylaxis and therapy for decubitus ulcers. The general nursing is easier for the patient, as well as for the nursing staff. The seriously ill patient can be moved without any effort from the supine position into the lateral position, which means that the patient is relieved from pain because the water mattress directly adjusts to the surface of the body.

Veerpleeghuis Zuiderhout Hospital, Harlem, Holland (Report by 7 staff members)

"All patients found lying on the bed comfortable and experienced much less pain, and were more rested because of improved sleeping; patient turning is not necessary."

The temperature control is beneficial and the bed cannot cool down with the patient on it. In addition, the patient can have a comfortable temperature to avoid perspiration.

No new Decubitus Ulcers developed when lying in the bed and existing Decubitus Ulcers improved very rapidly.

The waterbed is very important for dealing with Decubitus Ulcers, especially for those patients who cannot be treated in an ordinary way. This bed is suitable and necessary for prevention of Decubitus Ulcers, for patients in poor condition especially terminal care cases. Considerable nursing treatment time can be saved. Serious or persistent Decubitus Ulcers can be treated successfully.

Centre for Post Traumatic Paraplegics, l'Institution Nationale, Des Invalides, Paris, France (Dr G Lagrave, Head of Surgery)

"A recently handicapped tetraplegic was admitted with multiple sacral and trochanteric sores. Placing the patient on this bed proved to be beneficial for his comfort without any of the side effects which occur with simple water mattresses ("Sea Sickness", irregular floating sensation). Thanks to this particular flotation therapy the sores have healed without the need for surgery."

A paraplegic patient with multiple sacral and trochanteric sores as well as heel sores, was able to rest very easily on this bed. The sores were seen to improve, and functional re-education by mobilisation and physiotherapy was effected without difficulty."

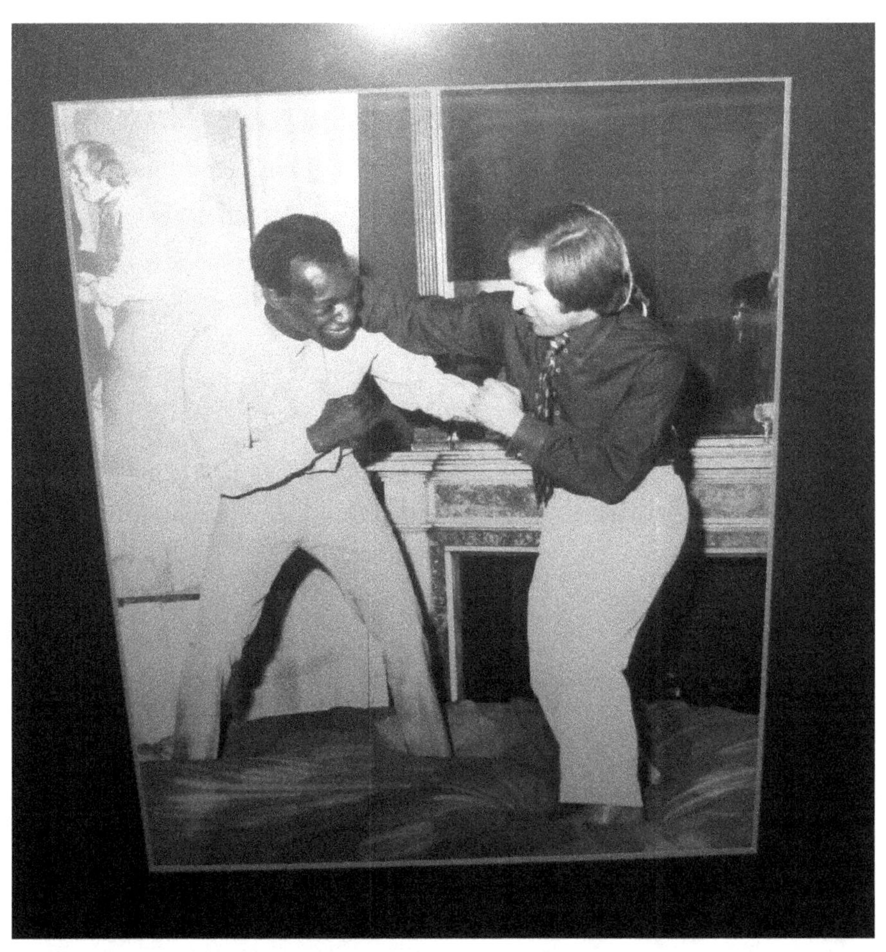

Care for a Little Sparring on a Waterbed?

Alon, a.k.a. Rocky appears for Western Medical

To do a little PR with Bunny Sterling,
Lightweight Champion of Europe

FINANCIAL TIMES

Top

The view from Alon's Parisian apartment

Left, The Camargue, France
Houseboat #2, 1993

Top Left, Alon relaxes aboard with *The Financial Times*

Bottom Left: Alon getting the houseboat through the mighty lock of the story, second largest to one in Russia.

A Tiny Sampling of Art, Chez Mintz

"I don't really know who drew this sketch of Ernest Hemingway. Carol and I both just know that we liked it."

The view from the living room ...

"Trigger"

Showcasing just a few objets d'art Alon and wife Carol find to be sources of great pleasure.

Above, Pen and Ink from Israel

Left, horse by Terrie Reid Kvenild,
art restorer and artist from Carmel, CA

Husband and Wife

Carol and Alon at Their Wedding
September 7, 1997

At the Black Cat Club in Cannes

1980'S

Alon and brother Steve in the Philippines,
outside Manila,
during a time out from business for Alon

DUBAI ... 1980

It was at a medical symposium and exhibition in Dubai, part of the United Arab Republic, that my distributor came to me and said, "What we really need is a burns system. The women here all cook with oil and are not careful, and so many of them get scalded by the oil. If you could develop a system or unit to deal with that I would buy hundreds of them. The cost almost doesn't matter."

I heard him clearly and went back to my London factories with that thought ringing in my ears. But it takes time, ideas and of course funds to develop new products. My staff and I worked months to come up with a product that could do the job. Then Fate intervened.

I was holding in my showroom what they call in England an "open day": we invited other companies to join with us to show off new products. I had a facsimile of a burns unit, but I knew it wasn't good enough. During the show I noticed a group of men standing around my partial burns system. I introduced myself and was told they were from the London Hospital for Tropical Diseases. They had been commissioned by the Minister of Health of Saudi Arabia to develop a machine that would keep the Hajji's safe, that is, those Muslims that had to make a pilgrimage to Mecca at least once in their lifetime. The Hajj moves forward a week every year and now it was in late March. Temperatures were already over 100 degrees. Many of the faithful were dying every year of heat stroke, and when even hotter weather descended in July and August, heat stroke victims would number in the thousands.

The group from London Hospital for Tropical Diseases had been commissioned to invent a system that could treat both heat stroke and burn patients. However, as much as academia knows, the planners didn't get their math correct and were absolutely not able to complete this task within budget.

When they saw my burns unit, they said that "Joined with our work ... possibly equipment produced by this company could give the Saudis what they require!" The problem of course was money. Saudi had lost faith in the institution and new funds were required to complete the project. My company was doing OK, meaning the bills were paid on time. If I were to start a new research and development project it would certainly put me deeply in debt. But it was a great challenge and one that if there was any way to accomplish, I wanted to jump on.

I got the name and phone number of the Minister Health in Saudi Arabia and actually called him. I was indeed brazen in doing so, but he answered the phone himself. I wasted no time and filled him in on all that had transpired. He said that he would be in London the following week on other business and we should meet. We did finally at 5:00 p.m. one day. He viewed the two systems and listened to how, working together, our two organizations could provide him with what the Kingdom needed. Later that evening, we ended up at a marvelous Italian restaurant where the Minister and I both drank a great deal of red wine. But I knew I had made contact!

A week later he called me from Riyadh, the capital of Saudi Arabia, and agreed to extend the finances we required. I was on a roll and now needed my suppliers to go along with me. More wine ... and they all agreed. What a crazy time.

We made two prototypes, both in unattractive stainless steel. But they were physically correct, with over 1000 holes in the parts that would give the heat stroke patients plenty of warm water on their bodies. In the past, heat stroke patients were placed in baths with ice, to lower their temperatures. That worked with some and gave heart attacks to most of the others. Ice closed their pores. No air, no life. Our idea was quite the opposite. Give them warm water to open their pores and allow the heat to gradually be released from their skin. Voila...it worked! Over two hundred pilgrims were saved.

Everyone there and in London was ecstatic. The Minister called me and his only complaint was that they were not attractive enough. I said I could do them in white fiberglass with rounded corners and even emboss the Saudi Tree Of Life on them! He actually screamed, "Yes, yes, yes!"

Obviously, I knew there would be a negotiation on price, so as everyone else does, you raise it ... and then reduce it, to please the buyer. The Minister ordered over 200 units at over $25,000 each. I was invited to fly to Saudi Arabia and meet with the king, who would personally sign the contract. They were even going to build five hospitals, specifically to house what would now be known as B.C.U.'s. (Body Cooling Units.) The Saudis called them "The Mecca-Mukarramah B.C.U." My ship had come in! NOT.

Early the next morning on the way to my gym for my usual daily workout, I walked into a car! No, a car did not hit me. I HIT THE CAR. I didn't see it. Something was amiss with my vision. Fortunately, I wasn't injured and just dusted myself off and moved on. At the gym, I was feeling odd but passed it off. On the way to my office, a few streets further on, I again had an unusual feeling. I called my personal physician and arranged a brain scan. Which was not easy to do in those days. But I had a very strange feeling about this and needed a resolution. The scan showed that I had a growing brain tumor. It needed to be operated on urgently. Of course it did ... but I had to be in Saudi Arabia for my ship that was coming in.

They said Professor Ponsford, the number one brain surgeon in England, would be dealing with me. I smiled and said lovely, but that I wasn't available for perhaps a week. I had to be in Saudi Arabia, as there were a great many people that needed to be paid.

Once they grasped that I was actually serious, they gave me a vile of tablets and said that if I felt my head actually expanding, I was to take one every two hours and get back to London as quickly as possible. They also said that I was a fool to allow money to take precedence over my life. I have no idea why, but I did not give it a second thought. I told no one. That was a bit difficult, but I just didn't want pity or comments or even ideas from others. I just wanted to get that contract. I admit that today it seems absurd, but then many things do in a lifetime.

When my plane landed in Riyadh, the Minister of Health was there with a limousine and a smile. He was full of himself and made jokes and told stories, but at some point he noticed I was not my usual self. He pushed me and I gave in and told him about the brain tumor, then showed him the pills. Instead of going to my hotel where I thought we were headed, we went to his office. I don't know if he spoke to the king himself or an associate, but instead of waiting perhaps five days to be seen, I was to be the first person he would see in the morning. Immediately after, a plane would fly me back to England.

The next morning is somewhat of a haze. I know I was collected at the hotel, the king signed the contract and I flew home.

Two days later Professor Ponsford removed my benign three inch brain tumor. That very day that Mrs. Margaret Thatcher, the Prime Minister, and Parliament, it was rumored, decided that hospitals did not need heat at night. So ours was cut off. I was on a flotation bed that I actually manufactured. I had heat. But the cold dropped down into almost freezing temperatures. Those with tracheotomies, breathing through plastic pipes inserted in their throats, found them seizing up, until no air could go through. Others with problems could not raise their voices or push a button to call attention to the very limited nursing staff. At least five men died that night. As did three women next door. That story was never released. You're the first to hear it. The only reason? To save a bit of money.

* * *

My brother and mother flew in from the United States to be by my side before the operation. Imagine their shock when Professor Ponsford came in extremely upset, and stated that it would be at least 24 to 48 hours before the heat could again be turned on. He asked if I could have nursing care at home. I immediately said yes and he replied that in his entire history, he had never sent a patient home the next morning after major brain surgery. However, he felt that it was the wisest move we could make under the circumstances. To the best of my knowledge the heat was turned on almost three days later. No publicity about further fatalities. Under the National Health plan, it is rare for anyone to even consider suing the government. They may have paid for burials, but that would have been all.

* * *

I had attempted to convince the Saudis that all machines require spare parts and as these units would be sitting in desert hospitals for months, unused and untouched until the hot weather returned, they would especially need spare parts. It would be best to order them at the same time the major order was being produced. Otherwise, when they needed them in the future, it would take three to four months to manufacture the necessary items.

Dollar rich and penny foolish, they refused. During the next Hajj all the units were there, installed and perfect, saving thousands of lives. However, the following year, they discovered that many had deteriorated from lack of use, as I predicted. They called and wanted to order parts immediately and were told it was just not physically possible. So they scavenged parts from other systems and at the end of that Hajj, were down from over 200 units to less than 70. I dread to think of what the future will bring, but I'm certain it will be a disaster. They will be attractive white fiberglass bodies with mechanisms that are useless. The five hospitals will likely be abandoned or used for other purposes. And when next summer arrives, bodies will again be stacked high.

Call it a misuse of the kingdom's funds or whatever, but for me, when the program started it was one of the most exciting and rewarding times in my life.

And the good news for me is that I still have a life. Thanks to a man who made a phone call to a king… and a surgeon who did his job successfully.

THE INSPECTOR
ABOUT 1980 ... LONDON ... THE EAST END

Jimmy O'Sullivan called me about midday at my office. He had been with Western Medical Group about ten years and had actually been my first employee in England. An all-around Man Friday, he was involved in most aspects of manufacture, deliveries, warehousing, and managing the other staff who worked in the various factories and shipping depots. Eventually, his father Tommy came on board in packaging; not a young man, but honest and as strong as a mule. It was somewhat unusual for Jim to ask to speak to me, as he mostly dealt with the office staff on his own. I took the call and he said in a shaky voice, "Gov'nor, I'm at the warehouse. You need to be here soon!" When I asked what was wrong he said that there was a fire truck and the police and fire agencies were on the scene.

It only took me a few minutes to catch a black cab, and I got to the scene rather quickly. There were indeed all sorts of uniformed officials present, along with a fire truck and police cars. My staff all had their heads down, looking crestfallen. I looked away from them and introduced myself to the men in uniform. Spotting my nice suit, waistcoat, and tie, a group of red-faced large men wearing scowls on their faces approached me. One stepped forward and said, "I hear you're a Yank?" I smiled a bit, and said, "Yes, I'm American, but I've lived here for ten years building this company." Then he bellowed out, "Do you get your money from insurance companies?" I replied that I had absolutely no idea what he was talking about, nor did I have a clue why I even had to be there. I heard a clink and saw a policeman staring at me, holding a pair of silver handcuffs. I took a deep breath and said that it would certainly be helpful if they could tell or show me what it was I was supposed to have done. Looking directly at him, I said, "I believe you may have made one serious mistake already." I had raised my voice an octave or two, which certainly got the attention I'd wanted. "OK, Yank, follow me," my questioner commanded. Turning to the policemen nearby, he added, "I want men on each side of the Yank, and behind him as well."

Flanked by my police escorts, I went to a staircase in the middle of the weather-worn old brick building, and climbed to the second floor. Immediately the odor of something that had been burning hit me. Now there had to be at least five of my staff and twenty police and firemen. I said to all of them, "Obviously an odd smell is in the air. What is it? Where is it coming from?" I had no idea whatsoever.

Our company supplied water mattresses and water cushions to hospitals for decubitus ulcers, or bed sores, as I've mentioned earlier. These items, laid out on the floor, were made of plastic. There were also high, neatly stacked piles of foam. Some fiberglass beds were there as well, being cleaned for reuse. The Inspector walked past me and pointed out a number of burns on various products. "A good thing the sprinkler worked, or this would have spread to other warehouses, which hold materials that could blow up an entire complex!" He was now almost screaming. This was absurd and it did not take me more than a few seconds to turn my own glaring eyes on him and raise my own voice. I asked that everyone step closer as they had made a major mistake. "The policemen and perhaps a few firemen should gather here," I added. "This was certainly arson. However, whoever did it was an idiot and had very little knowledge of these products." I sensed that I had them in my hand and played it out to the fullest. "First of all, Inspector, you spoke of my collecting an insurance claim. That is total nonsense! Why? Because I don't have a penny's worth of insurance on this warehouse! You see, if you had known the facts you would not have wasted so much time and manpower on this fiasco."

I turned to Jim O'Sullivan. "Jim, have you got your lighter with you?" I saw in his eyes that he now understood. He was managing a faint smile. "Please take a mattress and light it up." The firemen made guttural sounds. I was beginning to feel like Sherlock Holmes, right out of Scotland Yard. Jim held the flame directly to the mattress. The fire singed it, burned it, but these was not a flicker of a flame! "Jim, please do one of those pads, and the foam and any other product you see." He did so. Afterward, some materials had a black scorch mark, but there was not even a hint of fire.

I turned to the big man and the others in the crowd. "In England, hospitals have the strictest codes against any product that could be at all flammable. If these cannot burn, why would I need costly fire insurance? No, gentlemen, this was indeed done for a purpose, and I'm sure the fact that it didn't work upset the person who tried to create a fire."

I then turned to Tommy O'Sullivan. "Tommy, when you left last night, was everything locked up?" He put his hand through his wisp of white hair, thought for only a moment and said in his delightful Irish accent, "Now that you mention it, I don't honestly know. I was feeling a bit poorly and mentioned it to the new lad, Stuart. He said for me not to worry as he had some paperwork to do and would lock up when he left. That was about 4:30." I had only met the young man once, and at this point asked him to step forward. My first thought was to smack him, but instead I put both of my hands to the sides of his face and quietly, simply asked, "Why?" He crumbled in front of everyone. His girlfriend had just broken up with him, saying he would never amount to anything. He explained that he thought if he was involved in something big, she might view him differently. As he had only been working a few weeks there, he hadn't yet learned that everything was fire retardant. Tall and thin, he looked totally done in as he broke down and cried. I looked at the policeman with the handcuffs and said he could now put them to use. He shook his head sideways; it seemed that he and most of the others felt sorry for poor Stuart. In the end, the young lad received a year's probation.

The Inspector said, "Well, I guess that's it then. We can all head back." But at the bottom of the steps my ire got the best of me. I raised my voice and slowly said, "That's NOT it. Twenty minutes ago I was accused of arson by you for the insurance money. That officer was about to place cuffs on me. I could have done this in court and made you to look like a fool. How many times did you refer to me as 'the Yank'? YOU were the person in charge. You were also the judge and jury and I was certainly guilty. Throw away the key. Do you call that good police work? And now … now you don't even have the conscience, the human compassion for another whom you wronged. You just don't have the balls to even apologize!" Even outside you could hear a pin drop.

"What do you want, to sue us?" the Inspector asked me.

I looked at him with disgust. The big man saw it. "No, I have no intention of taking any such action against you. Oh, but I do want something." I hesitated, then resumed. "However, I don't believe you have enough balls to give it." His eyes and mouth showed he was completely aghast. I turned my back and started to walk away. "WHAT?' the Inspector now bellowed. I stopped and turned. All the men were still there, fixated on this conflict. I stared, nodded, and yelled back, "AN APOLOGY! For everything."

One would have thought I'd asked for his first born, as he actually shook. I waited a full minute and finally heard him whisper, "Sorry." I must have had fire in my eyes. "'Sorry' is not acceptable. This entire situation was pathetic and you can only say, 'Sorry?'"

There were strong men in that yard, but they were all moved by what was taking place in front of them. I was on a roll. "You would have locked me up in prison for years and bragged of your great police work. In hindsight perhaps there is something I should insist upon. All those others in dark prisons, fellows that YOU put there. Now one has to wonder how many INNOCENT people have lost their lives because of you. Incompetence? I would not bet against it. If your cases are reopened and examined, how many people would be let free with apologies?"

I could now see the firemen start to move toward their cars and trucks. The policemen, however, stood transfixed. I wondered what they were thinking, so I looked directly at them and asked. "You are living witnesses. Have you never wondered how the Inspector rose to where he is so quickly? Perhaps 95% of the men and women today behind bars should be there thanks to him, but if one of your family was in the other 5%, wrongly there because of this man, what would you do? It's not just myself, it's all these fine people I employ here, and our families and reputations. Is he a bad cop or was this a truly rare mistake? I have no idea, but I hope to God you will ask yourselves that question and file a report telling the truth, the facts, and hand it in at your office tomorrow. The newspapers would love this story. *The Daily Mail, Telegraph, The*

Times. Front page stuff this is." Many of their faces looked contorted and I knew when to get off my pulpit, and that whatever happened, I likely would never know. At this point I looked at the Inspector and he reminded me of young Stuart the arsonist, not quite as broken, but wounded.

I turned to Jim, "How about a ride back to the office for a Yank, mate?"

"Guv'nor, the honor will be mine."

As we walked to his van the Inspector looked at me and almost extended his hand to shake it, perhaps to really offer an apology. But he dropped his arm, withdrew and walked away. We could just grimace a bit in a draw between sadness and bitterness.
It was almost a year later, walking home from my office, that a man approached and introduced himself as Inspector Riley. He said, "I have some news for you, Sir. I was in that warehouse yard that day when you were falsely accused. There were a number of us that took your words very seriously and we did look into the records, and did write up a truthful report. In fact, there was more than one report submitted, which certainly got the attention of the high command. That individual is no longer with Her Majesty's Police." He shook his head, shrugged his shoulders and asked if I would accept his hand in an apology. "No," I commented, "Not in an apology, but yes, I would be delighted to shake your hand." He smiled and asked, "How about a good English beer?" I returned his look and replied, "Only if it's cold." We laughed, went to the pub and not a further word was spoken about the incident.

We met a few times after that. He was bright, and had a human way about him. Which just proves you can't judge the tree because of one bad apple.

GREECE AND FUN EXPERIENCES

I've been asked to write a story that is a bit "naughty." Although I'm not yet prepared to get too risqué, this is a real fun incident that took place some years ago.

My girlfriend at the time was Sherry. Blond and very attractive, with a marvelous figure. This was the era of women burning their bras. She was no exception. I was going off to the Middle East and Greece and she said she wanted to travel with me. I enjoyed her and not just because of the physical side. She was bright, a non complainer, had a definite interest in travel and perhaps most of all, a great sense of humor. She could tell jokes as well as any standup comedian. I agreed.

We made our way to Athens for a few days and then went to the seaport of Piraeus, where it was our intention to find a ship that would take us to the Greek Islands. The one called Hydra was the most interesting as a number of people had recommended it. But first we found a mid-size, inexpensive but clean hotel just a few streets from the port. We had intended to explore the area for two nights. I enjoy seaports as I can usually find a fresh fish restaurant there. The first night was enjoyable and we were told to be at the docks early to find a ship that would take us. The next day we walked and took in all there was to see in the area. Sherry stubbed a toe so when we saw a pharmacy we went in to buy some bandages. While there she saw a large chocolate bar and immediately bought that as well.

We had an early dinner and retired to bed as we wanted to be at the dock at first light. Here I add we still had almost a full bottle of wine, so we were pleased to call it an evening. Between finishing the chocolate bar and wine, everything was marvelous.

Or so we thought.

Almost in unison, at about 5:30 in the morning we woke up. Something was definitely wrong. We were unable to leave the bed immediately as we were ... I say this in the nicest possible way ... defecating or doing number two at the same time and non-stop, in the bed! A thought crossed my mind and I reached for the now empty chocolate bar wrapper. Although everything was written in Greek, I could easily see the word X-LAX! I explained to her that this was what one took when their bowels were not operating properly. And even then, just a very small piece the size of a quarter would be enough to make a person regular again. We had consumed an entire large bar of it, not even leaving a crumb. As I said earlier, she had a sense on humor and understood that we were certainly in a predicament. We had to stay in bed another half hour and let nature take its course. After which we cleaned and washed the bedding as best we could. It was diabolical and hysterical. I had paid the hotel bill the night before, so after giving everything a spring cleaning and opening every window we left as though everything was wonderful. But our journey was not over.

We almost ran to the docks, and began asking about a ship to Hydra. We came across one fellow who had a huge smile when he saw Sherry in a white T-shirt with no bra. He was very helpful, wrote a note and told us which ship to take. The note, in Greek of course, was just saying we were old friends and to please assist us. We went to the ship and the captain was there. He read the note and looked at Sherry's T-shirt.

We made introductions and he said he would be pleased to take us. That we should board now, as he was departing in only a few minutes. She said, "What great luck!" I only wondered. We went downstairs to the passenger quarters which were quite sparse. But as we knew it was not a long sail, and the captain said that there would be no charge because we knew his friend, we didn't complain.

A few minutes later the ropes were untied, the anchor pulled up and off we went. The odd thing was that we were the only passengers on the ship. Or so we thought. A few minutes later two policemen came down with hands on their weapons. Then we heard chains rattling and more footsteps. When we looked up, we understood it all. Each man was chained and carrying a very heavy black cement ball. As each entered our area they looked at Sherry's T-shirt and the remarks came. Fortunately they were in Greek. Nevertheless, it was not difficult to understand what they were referring to. YES, we were on a ship transporting gangsters, murderers, and terrorists to an island they would spend the rest of their lives on. They would only see their girlfriends or wives one day a month, forever. To them, this braless blond was their last joy. Needless to say, the captain approached us and said these men still had money on them and if…I stopped him there. I said it was a funny joke and we enjoyed it. But we were told that he was a man held in high esteem and respect, to not destroy that image. Furthermore, we were to be married shortly and we would not consider anything indecent. She was a good Catholic virgin and just the thought of it has made her ill. Actually it was the X-LAX still in her body, and she really did look pale and was trembling. However, about an hour into the sailing, she had established a chatting relationship with a few of the prisoners who spoke some English. She had borrowed a thick jacket from the captain and was much more comfortable. With an armed policeman she visited them all. They begged for one kiss but received only a warm smile for their families. When we docked at the island where they would be held, most, not all, gave the two of us a nod and a small smile. They understood that the captain was just trying to have a bit of fun.

The ship took us to Hydra where we spent a lot of time laughing. We made some friends and they heard about both the X-LAX and the ship. We were minor celebrities and had our 15 minutes of fame. Oh, yes. Before we left the ship I noticed a Greek calendar on a wall and asked if I could have it, as a memento of our voyage. The captain smiled and handed it to me. I had it framed and even today, it is on our kitchen wall.

BANGKOK TO MANILA ... ABOUT 1982

There was an expression, before 9/11, called by English check-in desk people, "Have a go." Simply put, if you arrive a bit late for your flight, but the doors of the plane have not quite closed, you were to run until your lungs were on fire and your legs gave out, in hope that the doors of your flight were not yet closed. My engineer and friend John Tichener and I had arrived at the airport in Bangkok late, due to a traffic accident that delayed our taxi. We were booked to fly from Bangkok to Manila, in the Philippines. Racing down hallways and corridors to the correct gate entrance, we were met by two smartly dressed flight attendants who had a good laugh looking at us. We were wearing suits and ties and oh, so business-like. They said the ticketing desk had called and said two "Have a goes" were running like mad to make the flight. The pilots were kind enough to hold the plane for the few extra minutes.

Once we were on board, the attendants said they had a few surprises for us as we were late. They asked what we wanted to drink after water and juice. John said Vodka. Then we were told we would be given full bottles, as they would seldom come over to visit us during the flight. We were perplexed. Also we were now to be in special seats. Our original seats had been given away to stand-by passengers. They led us to the back of the plane, where we were all curtained off. There were three seats. One was already occupied by a middle-aged man. He was on the aisle. We took the two seats, middle and window. John looked at me and we knew something was amiss. That's when we noticed he was wearing

handcuffs. Also he was a deathly shade of yellow. Words cannot express our emotions. But we knew he wasn't going anywhere soon and felt it would be better to befriend him, rather than aggravate the situation. Very bizarre. When the drinks came, we got an extra cup to share with him. Indeed he was grateful.
He said he had been arrested for smuggling, illegally as it was totally politically motivated, and he had languished in a Thai Prison for almost five years. He contracted a jaundice of some sort and that's when they decided to let him go back to the Philippines. Normally a guard would accompany a prisoner, but when the man who was to serve that function saw us boarding, he left. Clearly we were to be the on-board "guards."

The prisoner was actually very friendly and we became somewhat comfortable with him. But always on the alert. He shared stories of his life and John told him of our medical exhibition, which was to take place in Manila in a few days.

When we landed, some police took the man away and we thought that was it, just another story in life. The exhibition began and was typical of what they usually were. But Mrs. Fernando Marcos, yes, the President's lady, came by. She was lovely and bought everything we had shipped. Then, our airplane companion appeared, with his entire family. He introduced us to all of them. They thanked us for assisting him on the flight and were quite nice. His color had already begun changing and he was kind enough not to shake hands with us, as he understood we would not be comfortable with that. He also whispered not to leave anything with Mrs. Marcos without being paid in advance. A sixth sense told me to believe him. She never did pay. But a Pilipino company we never heard of transferred the entire sum due to my company, Western Medical. I had the equipment released to them. One never knows who one is sitting next to, on an airplane.

THE BEGINNING OF THE END
A STORY NEVER TOLD TO MORE THAN A FEW

London, 1983. I was told Mr. Michael Vanner was on the phone. He was head of Allied International Bank in London. For some years my Western Medical Group had enjoyed the bank's services. Vanner and I shared some small talk, then he announced he was leaving the bank for quite a plum job — to become Chief Financial Officer of a public company. I was sorry to see him leave. He was always helpful to me, and was becoming a personal friend as well.

We had a few lunches together over the next year and I was always pleased that Vanner still took such a keen interest in my group of companies. Later I was to discover there was another reason. Grovebell PLC, the firm he was joining, had bid on purchasing a few other companies, but was always rebuffed. Rumor had it that this was because the chairman and major stockholder, a Mr. Vasant Advani, from a wealthy Indian family, was not especially liked. It seemed he had a huge ego.

A few months after he had joined Grovebell, I read in the London Financial news that Grovebell had bid higher than others to acquire two firms, but even so the bid was rejected. Obviously this was upsetting to the board of Grovebell, and particularly to Mr. Advani. That is perhaps when Michael Vanner received his new order.

The call came through from him at the end of the day. Would I kindly do him the favor of having lunch at the company's headquarters in the City of London, with Mr. Advani and a few others. In fact it turned out to be their entire board of directors. I thought quickly and said I would try to cancel meetings the next day and would return his call shortly. I was gifted in that I had an accountant named Stanley Michaels. A wonderful man with many children, from an orthodox Jewish family. He had my greatest respect for many reasons. I called him and he agreed to join me at lunch in the imposing Grovebell Building the next day. I had a feeling that I was going to be pounced on and wanted an ally that I could completely trust. There was no one better in the world for this post than Stanley, who had been with me for well over 20 years and knew my companies well.

Instead of driving, he arrived as I requested by black taxi, and I joined him inside so that we could talk on the way to the meeting. I had an odd thought that this might not be a simple lunch. It was in the cab that I told him that Vanner had requested I bring not only my last set of accounts, but perhaps my future order book, which he was aware contained considerably more sales than ever before. In the back seat I explained that I had also read the negative article in *The Times* about Vasant Advani. He looked and smiled at me and said that although they might be interested in purchasing a profitable company, this was never done without due diligence and much more investigation. To this day I clearly recall saying, "Stanley, you are very likely right. However, I have a gut feeling that Michael Vanner was trying to tell me something, without saying the words. My question to you, as no one knows more, is IF, just IF...I am asked to name a price for my companies, what is that figure?" I thought he was going to smile or even laugh, but he heard the seriousness in my voice and viewed the expression on my face. He hesitated and then opened his briefcase, took out my accounts and a small calculator. The taxi fortunately had to stop at a few lights, allowing us more time. Finally, Stanley looked at me and said, "You are very premature. I am surprised that you of all people would even think an offer could be made this quickly." I adjusted my tie, then he smiled and did the same, as he held the numbers on the machine up for me to see. "Next year," he said, "you could ask for perhaps 25% more, the way the company is going." I memorized the numbers, thanked him and we went into the building.

As we walked in, Vasant Advani came out and introduced himself. Tall, heavyset, slicked black hair and a suit from Saville Row, shining of mohair. Large gold cufflinks, silk shirt, thick knotted tie, skin slightly dark and well attended. He was the personification of success. I felt an immediate wariness of this man, as did Stanley. Michael Vanner had obviously told them that I did not eat meat and we were served a fine salad, followed by a perfect salmon. Later I saw the company's in-house kitchen and was nothing short of envious. After we finished lunch he told us of his group's growth, their stock and value, which he pointed out were rising all the time. We finished with Port and Cognac. Then we were invited into his private office. Huge and imposing. Stanley looked at me. We both knew this was a demonstration to impress us. But why? He showed us photos of their other companies, intermingled with films of projects that they were taking on, costing millions of pounds sterling and in numerous countries. We were invited to spend time with the board members, none of whom impressed us. They imported automobiles into England, and millions of umbrellas and cloth from many countries. The list was endless. Stanley and I drank water now, as we started to understand why this was happening. Time can often pass quickly. It was now almost 6:00 p.m. and Advani said that as we were all having such a congenial time, let's have dinner here! Stanley needed to call his wife and explain we were in a long but serious meeting. Somehow I was not surprised when they had sea bass for me, and poured copious amounts of fine wines. The chef must have been told to bring the food slowly. We left the table almost at 1:00 in the morning. Vasant lit cigars which Stanley and I did not partake in, and opened a very expensive bottle of after dinner wine, putting on a good show.

I said it was really getting late and we all should be moving on. The members of the board looked exhausted. He said we should not concern ourselves as one of their cars would take us to our homes. Finally, I had had enough and whispered to him, "If you want a private talk, let's go somewhere and do it." He got the message and we went into yet another room. He explained that Michael Vanner had vouched for my company and how much he thought I had accomplished. Vasant was impressed, especially as he, too, was not born English. If I would join with them we could all see a brilliant future, he told me. I stated that if he was patient, in about a year my company could be worth perhaps double what it was now. I held in a smile when I watched him pour himself a double Scotch. This large man did not want to hear those words. "Look," he said, "We can pay you today what you might ask for next year. Name me a reasonable price and allow me to announce it for the financial markets tomorrow." Gotcha. I knew it!! Now was the time to make those acting lessons pay off.

I explained slowly that there were other companies very interested and that Mr. Michaels and I felt that a fair price was ..... Stanley's calculator in the taxi practically blinked in my mind. Very calmly, but stomach churning, I doubled that figure and added 10%. If this happened, he deserved that 10% as a reward. Advani grimaced as if he were going to faint. I offered, "Why not discuss this next year when we are worth much more with our vast order book?" Advani drank quickly and walked around the room, thinking but saying nothing. Finally, he spoke. "If I agree, can I announce this tomorrow to the press?" I said there was no difficulty with that whatsoever. However, if he did not deliver the agreed upon amount, plus other stipulations, then I would certainly need to report this to the press. He stood and grinned as if he were finally able to show all his doubters that he was for real. We had other matters to discuss. My title, the running of my companies, my present staff, presentation of accounts, my joining the main board, and many more items. Bless Stanley, he stayed, despite the fact that we went on until midnight of the second day. Numerous subjects were discussed, and agreements were reached. As we wrapped up, Stanley and I declined Advani's offer of one of their cars taking us to our homes, as we needed to talk in private. In the taxi we looked at each other, laughed and knew this was to be a night we would never forget. 12:00 p.m. one day to 12:00 a.m. a day and a half later. Life would never be the same.

Addendum

Advani and I disliked each other from the beginning. Michael Vanner and I could have bought Gillette Medical and brought it into the fold; Grovebell would have gained a true winner. But this idea was rejected by the Board. Just one of many. After about a year Advani asked me to meet with him in his office and said, "When do you want to leave?" I had expected this and had already appointed a law firm to represent me. I was pleased with the severance package, although I did wonder why he wanted to hold on to Grovebell so tightly, and why he did not ask me to make a counter offer.

Seven months later, living in a villa in Portugal, I discovered the reason. The dapper Mr. Advani sold invoices for goods delivered to a number of London banks. The problem was, they were the same invoices. He disappeared from England with over 15 million pounds sterling. By today's exchange rate, that's about 30 million dollars. He was last reported seen in Nigeria and Bombay. He cannot return to Europe. I can write my autobiography. I doubt he will ever write his.

* * *

YAHUDA'S DAUGHTER ... 1983

I flew into Tel Aviv for another medical exhibition, not very happily. I still did not have a distributor there, partly because I was very particular with the companies I dealt with. I always sought out special people and had not yet met one I felt comfortable with in Tel Aviv in the medical industry.

At the exhibit, we were displaying an incubator, a special bed for burns and various aids for the disabled. When the exhibit doors opened I spoke with numerous people but never felt any special closeness to one. A red haired fellow came by with a warm smile. I had seen other companies cater to him, only to discover that he and his brother owned the largest medical importing agency in the country. Competitors flocked to him, angling for his attention. I decided not to make an overt move. Which worked. He came to visit our booth. His name was Amos Gazit. We shook hands, and our smiles attracted each of us to the other. Admittedly, I had a ringer in my group; my mother was there. She had flown from Los Angeles to London and with little effort I had convinced her to join my engineer and me in Israel. Amos spoke English and was well educated, as was everyone in his family. Eventually he and I chatted about my products. He had nothing like them and was interested in representing my company, but explained he had a brother, his partner, who had to see them as well before he could make a commitment.

The next day Amos came by with his brother Yahuda, who began by welcoming my mother to his country. Then he turned to me and said, "Show me what has impressed Amos." I did, and he also became motivated enough to ask to represent us. The two Gazit brothers moved throughout the hall for a few hours and returned with a surprise. That night there was to be a small reception at Yahuda's home, and we were invited. Mom accepted for us, and I was so pleased to see her smile.

When we arrived there were perhaps twenty or so people and we were greeted by all, although we knew no one. We met children, adults, their office staff and others. The food was fresh, healthy and presented with kindness. Then Yahuda and his lovely wife brought their daughter Rona to meet us. Fifteen and so beautiful. We were stunned by her. She was to be a doctor and was amazing in every way. She bonded with my mother and told us what her father had told her of us and our products. We felt as if we were with family.

I never signed a contract with the Gazit brothers, just shook hands. A piece of paper was unnecessary. I could not have asked for better. As they were honest and superb in every way, I offered to give them a discount and was told to treat them as I treated other representatives. Wonderful.

I made a number of visits to Tel Aviv later, and always felt at home. Eventually, I met their two sons, who were brilliant. Rona was growing quickly into a top student and worked to learn all she could about medicine. Had she entered a Miss World contest, she would have won hands down.

I could not visit them for Rona's seventeenth birthday, but made plans to go a week later when I was to be in the Middle East. That's when I received the call from Amos.

Rona was at a children's camp, assisting young girls with disabilities. There had been a commotion of some sort and the young men took their weapons and spread out to see that there were no enemies about. There was a fatal mistake. They left no men in the campsite. Somehow other men came in unnoticed. Armed with knives and moving quietly, they slit the throats of all fourteen children, including Rona. There is no need to go into the shock that struck everyone afterwards. As is the Jewish custom, they were all buried shortly after they died. Amos suggested that I not come, as Yahuda and his entire family were in seclusion. Everyone was asked to leave them for now; it was a period for them to be alone in their grief. Obviously I asked as so many others did, what could we do? He said in time he would let us know. It would not be very soon, but to please honor this request. We all did.

Months passed and I heard nothing from Yahuda. But finally, broken in heart, he started to return to life. That's when I had an idea. I had developed a unique new bed system, for long term patients. It was costly as there was quite a bit of research and development to recoup. The small country of Israel could not afford one yet, but I decided it was time for them to have one. A special one. It was to be made in light blue and white fiberglass, the country's colors. There was also to be a very important plaque embedded into the front panel. I don't know if my staff had ever seen me as possessed about anything as I was about this. I related the story, almost in its entirety, and they felt my need and indeed my pain. Most were English, Irish and Scots. But this was not about religion; this was of far higher importance: children and their massacre.

I called Amos and told him I was sending a bed with Rona's name imprinted on it. He was extremely moved and told me to send it to his office, addressed to his name; he would place it in a particular hospital, devoted to children. He did not feel the time was quite right for Yahuda to see it. When it was, he would take him there personally. I never told my mother about Rona, as she adored this young girl and would have been crushed.

Some months passed and I heard nothing about the bed other than it was now in place. Then one day Amos asked Yahuda to accompany him to that hospital, as they had not seen him for so long and were always asking after him. Reluctantly he agreed. When the brothers arrived, they walked and spoke of various matters with some of the staff. Then a nurse came to Yahuda and thanked him for the wonderful gift. Having no idea what she meant, he asked to see it. When he did, Amos said Yahuda almost fell apart. He knew nothing about it of course. The company did not purchase it. Then he saw and read the plaque, "In memory of our beloved Rona Gazit, who is with the Angels. She will be in our hearts forever."

I saw Yahuda again after almost a year at a medical exhibition in Paris. He now was aware of what had taken place. About Rona, the children's hospital, with the "special bed" in her name. Without words, our eyes met. He slowly came up to me and we embraced. He nodded his head a few times and tried to say something, but could not. Nor could I.

He finally broke our tender silence. "She was an angel." I forced a smile through a tear and replied, "And we had the gift of that angel, for at least a while."

It was interesting that others who knew one or both of us never interrupted those moments. They understood and left us to each other. No doubt Yahuda had others who knew parts of the story of Rona. But I had the privilege and joy of actually knowing her. Yahuda and I passed each other on other occasions, smiled but never again spoke a word to each other. Those were just times that words were not necessary.

* * *

1983 ... SAM RAVEL ... LONDON, ENGLAND

Norman Stoller was the son of the owner and the new Managing Director of a large British healthcare company, dealing mainly in numerous types of bandaging products. His company, Seaton Products, had factories in Manchester and had been in business for a great many years.

A short man with a large ego, Stoller took a dislike to me almost immediately. He was one of the major Jewish philanthropists in the United Kingdom. I, on the other hand, traveled near and far, including just about every Arab nation in the world. I had a secondary passport under the name Ali Mintez. When he heard about that he thought it a disgrace for a Jewish man. But I was marketing health care equipment and aids for the disabled, and not dealing in weapons or products that killed. Many of my Arab distributors guessed that I was Jewish, but all recognized that I delivered health care, not death or destruction.

Around this time, there were very few medical companies managed or owned by Jewish people, so he and his company were rarities. When I appeared on the London scene, without much in the way of financial capital, and then was on the road to success in a few short years, he liked me even less.

Thus, I was quite surprised one day when my secretary informed me that Norman Stoller was on the phone asking to talk to me. My first assumptions were that he wanted money for a charity or to complain about something. But I never evaded a call and took his. "Alon, old boy, how goes it? I've heard some wonderful things about you!" I clearly recall closing my eyes and saying, "How kind you are!" He went on. "I know we don't see much of each other these days, what with you in the South and all the travel you do, whilst I'm stuck up here in the cold North. Perhaps we need to do something about that soon. Maybe a long weekend on my craft in the gorgeous Lake District?"

No doubt was in my mind now; he definitely wanted something. Nevertheless, I was very friendly and replied that it was a fine idea and to let me know when it was most convenient. A bit more small talk and then he came to the real reason he was calling. We shared the same distributors in Tel Aviv, Amos and Yahuda Gazit. Both brilliant and brave. An exceptional combination, and I was very pleased when they signed on with me. But this was not about them. They had given a gentleman Norman's name and mine to contact when the man required special assistance in London. Now was that time. He first went to Norman as his company was world renowned. I was a much smaller fish. However, the brothers knew me personally far better, through my contacts in the Arabic world, so now I was being asked to help, though I had no idea yet with what.

"I have with me a chap from Israel," Stoller continued. "A Mr. Ravel. Our mutual good friends there have given him our names as possibly being able to assist him. Obviously, I would like to. However, for various reasons I find his needs quite difficult. Plus, you could make his travel much easier since you're in London. The Gazit Brothers and I would appreciate it greatly … As will the State of Israel."

My interest and curiosity were indeed piqued. If he was passing something like this on to me, it obviously was not a situation he wished to be part of. Without hesitation, however, I replied that I would be pleased to meet with the man and if he would prefer to come to my offices after 7 p.m. some evening, I could assure him of anonymity and privacy. When he connected to a speaker phone, I heard the man request the next night, if it were not inconvenient. I replied that even if it was, I would change my plans. He said, "Thank you" in English, with an accent. "Al-lo-davar," I said.

"You're welcome," in Hebrew. I imagined there might be a slight smile on his face.

The next evening, although my office staff usually stayed a bit late, I made a suitable excuse and they were all gone before my new adventure made his presence known. His name was Sam Ravel, slight in stature and a man who would not be noticed easily in a crowd. He would appear to be just another man, passing through life, which would in fact be anything but reality.

Sam was a longtime Mossad leader, based in Belgium and Paris, depending on the day and where he felt he needed to be. His previous contact in England had developed cancer and his time was very limited. Sam had an agent who needed to travel quite a lot, and required an identity that would be credible wherever he went. He would need business cards, brochures, leaflets, a knowledge of whatever product or service he would be associated with, and a phone number and address along with any other items that would serve to legitimize him.

Sam's agent spoke perfect English and would in no way compromise my company. He was to work on a straight commission basis and would be of no financial cost. I listened intently, and assuming Mr. Ravel was who he said he was and was employed by who he said he was, there was no doubt that I was prepared to proceed as his English contact, and I told him so. He asked that I call the Israeli embassy and ask specific questions. I could ask anything I wanted, he said, and recommended that I speak with someone of high rank. I called information as I wanted to be certain I had an honest phone number. When I received the number and called, I said my name and left my own phone contact, and was informed that someone would be calling within the hour. About 15 minutes later a diplomat called. I had been to the Israeli embassy twice before and knew the general layout of the place. I asked him to describe various rooms, and a number of other questions, including the names of Israeli cities and towns. I also asked who did they know that knew me. He not only answered each correctly, but proceeded to tell me when I had visited the embassy and why, and other details that he could not have guessed. If in fact I wanted to meet him there, he would oblige without question.

I asked Sam when I would meet the agent, whom I was to know only as David, and was surprised when he answered, "In two minutes, if you wish." We walked to the front door where Sam took out his pocket hanky and wiped his face with it. A young man waiting at a closed news kiosk stood reading a newspaper. When he saw us, he immediately put it down and crossed the street to join us. Tall and somewhat handsome, he spoke in Hebrew to Mr. Ravel, smiled and said to me in perfect English, "Shalom, Dr. Mintz, welcome to the club." It was not a long relationship, but proved to be one I would never forget.

"David" was remarkably intelligent and learned the inner workings of almost all of my products in a few short weeks. He was slightly remote and my engineers and other staff had to work a bit to get to know him. This was mentioned to me by a few people and I invited him for a very private dinner where we discussed it. He explained that he was taught not to make friends with people that he likely would never see again or who could become a problem in one way or another. I understood his reluctance but said that as he was quite a good actor, it would benefit us if he changed that persona and played his part a bit more warmly. He smiled and said a new David would be with us tomorrow.

He wasn't joking. Everything from his neatly pressed trousers to his somewhat dour disposition vanished and he became almost one of the staff immediately. I say "almost" as he informed me that within a week he would be moving on, into the field, where he could do what he was trained for. Not Western medical training, but rather that of the Mossad. He would make periodic visits to London to reestablish his contacts.

Time passed and on occasion I received a call from him just to touch base and hear of anything new that he should be aware of. But then on one Saturday night, at almost midnight, the phone rang, disturbing a lady friend and myself. Reluctantly, I picked it up. It was David.

"Alon, I'm on New Cavendish Street, three short streets away. I was going to call you tomorrow but I'm outside the Cavendish Hotel and feel I've been recognized. There are three, perhaps four men following me and I know they're from the other side. I'm very sorry to trouble you, but at this moment I've nowhere else to turn and I have no equipment with me." Meaning he was unarmed. He went on to say that he was near the archway of my building. He knew I lived nearby, but not only had he never been to my townhouse, he had no idea if I was alone. "Can you offer any assistance?" he asked.

I told him to stay where he was and I would be there in about five minutes driving a dark blue Jaguar. The rear door would be open and he was to go inside, keeping a low profile. I am and never was a special agent type; however, at that moment I felt I had no choice. I excused myself from the lady, put on jeans, a dark shirt and for the first time in perhaps twenty-five years, reached for a book on one of the upper shelves. I quickly explained I had a major buyer for it and I had no alternative but to show it to him. I doubt if she believed me, but she turned over and went to sleep.

Racing down the staircase, I knew I was possibly facing a very difficult situation. "In for a penny, in for a pound" crossed my mind. My car was parked just across the street and I was in it and speeding to my office in a very short time. I arrived in less than the five minutes I had told David, but already almost too late.

Whoever they were, they had seen him and shot in his direction. I bleeped my horn once and he saw me. For some reason he had a bit of a problem opening the rear door and I had to stop, get out and help him.

As I got the door open, I heard the sound of bullets and took my old revolver out of my book. I was a bit concerned it would explode in my face, but luck was with me. I heard David cry out — he was hit in the lower knee. I pushed him into the car, closed the door and emptied my clip of bullets directly at the place the shots had come from.

I heard one man cry out, then jumped into the driver's seat and drove carefully to a large packing facility I had. Nothing fancy, but I knew where one of the locker keys was and dragged David inside. There I found fabrics, and David and I worked together to bandage his leg. After some sips of water and a bit of tender care, he looked at me and made a remark about my not being just a medical businessman. I thanked him for the compliment and told him my real name was James Bond. It took a few seconds and then we both had a good laugh. He made a phone call from the small office, then put me on the phone. I spoke to someone I did not know, giving driving directions. He spoke to them again in Hebrew, then turned to me, saying they would be with us shortly. It was at least half an hour before they came, but that gave us a bit of personal time. Eye contact and a hug followed. These were truly emotional moments. A dark van finally arrived and David was carried away.

The next day Sam called to invite me to lunch. He embraced me and said that my work for the Mossad was done. Then he smiled and said that he never wanted Norman Stoller anyway. I was always their first choice. I could only smile. Apparently they had found someone else, not quite the James Bond character I had turned into, or so they guessed. I said that was fine with me as I was moving to Portugal. He smiled and said it was a beautiful country. I never saw either of them again to the best of my knowledge. But I must admit there have been times I looked over a shoulder, wondering if they were nearby, watching over me …

JUMP

At a guess it was 1984. I was a guest of the Thai medical military. A group of them was on their way to Pataya, a lovely island at the time. I was invited to join the Pataya-bound expedition as I had made a donation of beds to their hospital. It was a long, hot drive. When we reached their base I was assigned a room and invited to go to their beach. Basically it was very private, with ships and Chinese junks in front and a large bar on the beach. They all drank, and not to be difficult, I drank along with them. That was a major mistake.

A day earlier I had mentioned to their commander that I had completed forty-nine jumps from airplanes. Those were in America and in the best of conditions. I didn't think he would recall that conversation, but sadly he did. When we reached our destination it was party time. I will not go into detail, except to say that there was nothing missing.

The next day I was invited onto an airplane to reach number fifty! The booze was still pouring and I was about to start snoring, but agreed to go into the plane. That was not a clever decision.

We were about twenty thousand feet up when I felt the parachute being strapped onto my back. However, I was in a state of total relaxation and went along with everything. Foolish me. There came a time that I was hugged and placed in the doorway, then actually pushed off the plane. It wasn't long until I realized I was airborne. Immediately pulling the toggle line of the chute, I was tugged upward abruptly, then started a reassuring, moderately paced descent. As my vision cleared, I saw that I was about to crash into the harbor with the ships. I chose a place that looked reasonably safe, and pulled the line, allowing me to drop into the sea without hitting a ship. You can call it luck, it doesn't matter, but I fell between two large boats.

I swam under them and somehow came clear of any potential risk. Gradually I somehow made it to shore. I expected to be greeted warmly by everyone. But that was not to be.
The group had seen me jump, and pull my chute, and they all thought I had crashed into one of the ships in the water. Every single one of them, including the commander, leaped into the sea to try and rescue me. When I reached the beach and saw the bartender he was amazed. "Oh, they are all in the water to save you!" I asked for a beer and just waited for their return. When they came back and saw me, it was cheers and handshakes and lots of smiles.

Another day in paradise.

A BAD DAY ENDS UP OK ... STEVE

It was an early evening in August, 1985. I was reading, in the study at my home in Vale Do Garrao, which is a beach area in Portugal. Relaxed and calm, I was jarred by the ringing of the telephone. I walked into the kitchen to answer it. That telephone, for some inexplicable reason, always seemed to have the clearest line.

"Hello, Alon?"

"Yes."

"Alon, this may seem unusual as we have never spoken. I'm Gary Riches. The fellow that married your brother Steve's former wife."

I was truly baffled.

"Alon, I've been asked to make this call by the kids, as they're quite shaken right now."

Instantly my heart and mind were listening in disbelief, awaiting terrible news.

"Alon, we're at Saint Joseph's Hospital in Burbank. There is a possibility that your brother Steve may have had a heart attack. But that's not a certainty, just the first thought."

My brother has been my best friend since infancy. We're about three and a half years apart, as I mentioned at the beginning of this book. We argue like hell itself, and never need to say sorry. We've grown up very differently. He went into Air Force intelligence, residing at bases in the Philippines. I had a thirst for education, the theater and finance and went on to various universities in a number of countries. He lived a normal life playing quarterback for the Air Force team in the Philippines, until he was injured and returned to Los Angeles to become a super star in the eyewear field. He can do it all and has been a great success. Once a competitor called him a living legend. That was in Harry's American Bar in Paris, where I happened to meet a few people attending an eyewear exhibition.

A worldwide traveler, Steve's 6 feet tall, lean and eats everything. Handsome as a movie actor, and a dancer on top of it all! Whereas I hold to a strict fish, pasta and veggie diet. But he's had some internal difficulties, and I think now he's watching his food intake more carefully. He owns a lovely home in Woodland Hills, California, where he has been for over twenty-five years. He's single but goes out frequently to the theater and to dance. He has a son, Lonny, who is bright, handsome and successful. He's also gifted with a daughter, Jennifer, a few years younger and a graduate of Sonoma State. She's married to Robin, a CPA and accountant. A few months ago they had "AJ," Andrew James, a bundle of fun.

Our biggest argument I suppose is that with his success Steve and his pals have become Republicans! We battle royally, and when finally winded, change the subject to one we all can agree upon. He's still on pleasant terms with Sandy, his former wife and the mother of Lon and Jen. That's just a snapshot of Steve. Husband, father, businessman and even a hero. He's quite a man, and has a marvelous group of friends. I must add that he is not just a dancer, but a great dancer. I could write story after story about him.

My first words to Gary Riches were, "Thank you…thank you so much for making this call, which I understand cannot be easy for you." He responded with something polite and I concluded the conversation saying I needed to call the airport immediately before they closed. Whatever it took, I would be there and would he please tell my brother I was on the way. The Portuguese Algarve has a small but rather new and modern airport based just outside the town of Faro. I was fortunate in that I reached someone from the airport about 15 minutes before they closed for the evening. I explained with as much drama as possible what was taking place. The man at the airport replied that I could take the first morning flight. Although it was already full, he would get me on. I would then have a three hour wait in Lisbon before taking the Air Portugal flight to New York. He would even try to upgrade me to First Class. At the moment there was a connecting flight to Los Angeles, and although it, too, was full, he would get me on it. Was I prepared to pay First Class if required? I said, "This is my brother! I'll do what ever it takes." That upgrade would prove to be almost fateful.

The next morning I was early at Faro Airport to board the plane. In Lisbon I paced the floor, and had no idea what the situation was in L.A. There were only a few passengers in First Class and I was put into seat 1A. Many thoughts of my brother raced through my mind as the plane picked up speed toward take off. I adjusted my seatbelt, closed my eyes as the runway was starting to disappear, and then, "BAM!" We think and hope it's only imagination, but it's fractionally seconds when you understand that something is terribly wrong. In our case something was, in the rear luggage section of the plane. Five or ten minutes more and our liftoff would have been a nose dive down. The right wing, on my side, threw flames into the air. But the plane stopped and we were still on Terre Firma, Earth.

Lots of panic, screams and turmoil. However, the crew had rehearsed something like this. Rolls of strong cloth were hurled onto the airfield, women were told to take their high heeled shoes off. A female flight attendant was pushed by accident onto the runway, leaving only the two pilots and myself on board. For some reason all three of us were calm. It was as if we knew the terror was over. I don't think there was a dry spot on our faces. Sweat was thick and our tongues were dry.

When I went into the terminal we were told that the explosion was caused by ammunition that had been sent to troops in the field, accidently never unloaded and past a time limitation. If that was the truth I've no idea. All I knew was that I had to get to Los Angeles. The passengers on the plane were put up in local hotels, with meals and everything provided. All except one person: me. By this time the pilots and everyone else knew of my urgency and I was transferred onto another plane. I believe it was Continental. I was treated as someone important and again placed in First Class, where the cabin crew flooded me with attention. I always felt the First Class upgrade was a big part of the reason I was treated so well.

When we landed at Kennedy Airport in New York, I was whisked away and immediately placed on another flight to Los Angeles. When I landed, Carol's brother Warren was there to meet me. He drove quickly to the hospital and in no time, I was at my brother's bedside. He looked at me and smiled. "Rough flight?" I simply said it was somewhat eventful. He was in the middle of being given a hand bath by a lovely young nurse and looked as contented as I'd ever seen him. I mumbled, "But your heart attack?" He said it turned out not to be a heart attack ... just a blockage to an artery. No problem, they will have it as good as new shortly. Of course he was in an ebullient mood, as the nurse was continuing to bathe him. Then he said, "So what are you doing in the States?" He had no idea and to this day still doesn't. I don't care. He's still here!

1988 ... THE ALGARVE, PORTUGAL

About 2:00 a.m., on a very dark, deserted road about a mile from the beach and my villa. With Suzanne, my former short-term wife; we had three, perhaps four years of sort of togetherness. We just stayed with each other far too long. She was a classical blond ballet dancer. I worked hard, played hard and attempted to please more people than possible. Suzanne's sister and I had lived together in Europe and the States. Frankly, I preferred her. She had a better sense of humor.

In any case, we were coming from the latest discotheque in the Algarve, at Quinto do Lago. About two hundred sweating people drinking as if there was no tomorrow, dancing as if they had rhythm and acting like fools most of the time. But times were good and people were enjoying themselves. Then it came to a violent halt, almost ending two lives.

While we were driving to our villa, I insisted Suzanne put on her seat belt. She had had more than a few drinks and was not totally coherent. I attempted to take the wheel, but she became nasty and would not hear of it. Reluctantly I relented, a major mistake on my part.

As we sped down the unpaved, unlit and rough road, we suddenly saw a black car parked in the middle. I've no idea if it had run out of gas, or was left there for some other reason. Due to the speed of our car, Suzanne had no time to apply the brakes. She had three choices: turn right and crash into the white washed cement wall, go straight and smash into the car in the road, or turn left into the woods. I admit I would have done the same as she did, take my chance in the woods. A wrong decision, however. We hit a very large tree. The tree won the battle easily.

I vaguely recall the people trying to pull us out. It wasn't interesting or even frightening. I moved my feet and arms and understood there was pain that I could not quite understand in a few places. But I could think and reason and knew where I was. I heard Suzanne's cry, hurt but clear. Obviously there was a lot of blood, but I had bled before and really wasn't concerned by it. I don't recall if it was an ambulance or people's cars that took us to Faro Hospital. I do remember my right leg and hands starting to scream for release from their excruciating pain. I was placed on a metal trolley where I remained for hours. I started to raise my voice and was eventually taken to a bed where the sheets had not yet been changed from the last occupant.

The night was a blur and I passed out. I awoke to a room full of doctors. They all said the same thing, which I immediately rejected: cut the bottom half of my right leg off. I said, "Out of the question. I was born with these parts and intend to leave with them." After a brief discussion, it was agreed I would be taken, in their one leaking ambulance, the three or four hundred miles it would take to get to the major hospital in Lisbon. I mention this as there was pouring rain outside. They would also lend me a metal bedpan, if I needed to relieve myself. They so wanted to divest themselves of me. But they got the idea — amputation was out of the question!

With a driver who sipped whiskey from a bottle, the ambulance and I left early the next morning. Of course heavy rains persisted, and water poured into the back section where I was propped up on two ancient pillows I was attempting to relax on. I recall actually smiling at this ludicrous situation. We stopped two or three times in the next four hours so the driver could refill his flask. I even had a sip or two, which along with the pain medication left me almost grinning at my predicament. Was this real, or just a fantasy? When we drove into the parking area of "Our Lady of Jesus" private hospital, all doubts were erased from my mind. It was a small place, holding perhaps thirty patients. But somewhat elegant, perhaps once a charming residence. The nuns treated me kindly and I was taken gently into a private room. If the President were injured this is where he would go. There were only two beds in a room, and Suzanne had the other. A surgeon appeared and placed a titanium rod in her arm. Late that afternoon Suzanne was discharged and I neither heard nor saw her for the entire time I was in the hospital. We made no effort to contact each other. She realized her drinking and driving was the main cause of my condition. Any friendship we shared was no longer there. I was hospitalized for three months and one week! Eternity!!

Somewhere during my stay I learned I was in a private hospital for wealthy Portuguese individuals. Fortunately, I had insurance so that wasn't a problem, although there was one instance where the nuns wanted me to leave immediately for nonpayment of a bill. My own doctor, who spoke excellent English, asked about it and laughed. It was for the men who bedpanned me. The funny part was they never gave me a bill! I was supposed to ask every week what I owed them. How I was to know that I've no idea, as no one ever mentioned it. The grand total was less than one hundred dollars, so my doctor personally wrote them a check and just added it onto his statement to me, which was only a few hundred dollars. The day he sent the statement, my Portuguese bank paid him and instructed the nuns to bill them in the future. But for a few moments there, I was about to be evicted from "Our Lady of Jesus Hospital!"

When I finally did leave, my travel agency, hundreds of miles away, sent a limousine for me at no charge. I suppose I was a rather good client.

When my villa there was being constructed, I had designed a truly state of the art gymnasium and shipped it all out from London. Obviously, it was not originally installed for rehabilitation purposes, just to keep fit. But after the accident, I felt fortunate that the equipment was with me, and that I was able to locate a trainer who had previously worked in European hospitals. He was dedicated to helping me walk again, and came five days a week, two hours a day. He pushed and pounded me every minute and forced me far beyond any level I would have tried for without his persistence. Then he would massage my legs for a half hour. When he left I would be exhausted, but gradually I could see progress. I took no pain tablets. When the leg hurt badly, I just went to the pool, soaking up sun, and would slide into the water for at least two hours, trying to kick and move my legs.

It took eight long months before I went back to the first and second hospitals without a crutch or cane. I was walking normally, on my own two legs. I saw the doctors who wanted to amputate and did a little jig of a dance for them. Words were not necessary. However, that time still plays havoc with my mind, when I'm in a car.

THE 1990'S

Carol and Alon in Auxerre, aboard Houseboat #1

MEMORIES ... 1991

It was after twenty-five years of having homes in different places, and my main base in London, that I was able to successfully call it a day and build a new home in Portugal. The weather there is almost exactly like that of Los Angeles. And it, too, has nice beaches, along with fishing and people I feel comfortable with. When I moved there I became a permanent resident. A caring retired teacher gave me language lessons, and I made a sincere effort to have Portuguese friends, rather than other ex-patriots.

About a year after I moved in, a friend who had five adult children, all producing further kin, mentioned to me that his boat was now too small for his growing family. Not large, it could sleep two in comfort. Four could sleep aboard, but would be cramped. He was now going to purchase a much larger boat.

I knew what he was hinting at. After an evening at the Algarve Café, I became the owner of a 32 foot rather old and unattractive sea vessel. I had it sanded and repainted in red, white and blue. Not like the flag, but each color was distinct. Before long, all the locals and fishermen knew my craft. In the beginning, I was out at sea perhaps four days a week, catching just enough fish for friends, the beach restaurant where the boat was moored, and of course my own table, as that is mainly what I dined on most days.

I'm not a sailor. Never had a single lesson, so my sea journeys were always rather close to land. In time that became somewhat boring and I reduced my sea time to only a day or two a week, or when I just felt an urge to be away. In a town named Albufeira, there is a wonderful large fish market, half the size of a football field, with many vendors selling their wares — numerous varieties of fish and sea food — just brought in that morning by the dozens of boats that go out six days a week. The seafood choices available were more than anyone can imagine. It was far from an elegant market, on a beach with a tin roof and nothing on the sides to protect anyone when it rained. However, the fish were just caught, so fresh that no one stood on ceremony. The prices were right and you could even negotiate a bit, just for fun. Then one day the vendors went on strike. Their rent was raised to a figure they felt was unfair. Strikes are not uncommon in Europe.

Both Raphael, from whom I bought my boat, and I were in the market the day of the strike. He was on a holiday, which he seemed to take quite often. I think so many babies from his children were starting to play on his nervous system. We decided to have an early lunch together and walked up the many steps to the Ruina Restaurant, built over 100 years ago, above the fish market. No menu. What they had was what was just brought in by the fishermen. Because of the strike, the choices were limited. But we sat and smiled and ordered a plethora of food and of course marvelous Portuguese wine. The late morning seeped into the afternoon. We ate and drank slowly, enjoying our time.

Raphael asked me why I didn't just take the boat out and fish for my supper. I explained that I had a limited area that I could go in the sea, as I was not a sailor. He mulled that over for some time and then suggested that we take the "Yankee Clipper," my new name for the boat, and go fishing. He had boated all his life in the area and much further afield, and had a special freezer that could hold many kilos of whatever we caught. Also. he could bring another refrigerator that we could put next to mine and we could store vegetables and fruits. We could go five days, perhaps a week. For me this was an exciting experience, and immediately I said yes! He came to my house at 5:30 the next morning, in his van, now loaded down with foods and equipment. I supplied a box of wines, red, white and rose, along with ports for the cool evenings. Spices as well, as they add so much to the flavor to the fish. After all, I was to be the chef.

It was one of the finest times of my life. We caught fabulous fish, filleted them, cooked some on a small burner, ate at least half raw as sashimi. I even made some pasta. We read books, listened to music on my tape player and frequently dived into the clear blue water to keep us from getting too complacent and making any foolish mistakes. Could I have done another week or longer? I regret that I never had the opportunity to try. When our voyage was over, with buckets filled with delicious foods from the sea, we came back to more than reality.

The first place we stopped was at the restaurant, to give them a great helping of our catch. Then without even a discussion we went to Antonio's Bar and Grill, to see our pals and tell them of our trip. But as soon as we walked in, we could sense the atmosphere was different. Our friends looked at us, and admittedly, we had not shaved or showered, just swam. Our clothes were wrinkled, and altogether, despite our great sunburns, we looked tatty. Plus, we were carrying two buckets of fish to give to Antonio. We were more than a little surprised, though, at the reception we were given. Cold. Then one of our friends at the bar looked at us and asked if we had been out fishing the past week. We nodded yes. Then came the shocking words, "So you missed ... the war?" Obviously we had no idea what he was referring to. "Operation Desert Storm!" he told us.

In my book of life, in all my memories, the one that will stand out is that time when I was fishing while so many allies joined with America to form a coalition to stop Iraq from attacking Kuwait and Saudi Arabia. We sat at the bar and watched CNN on the television, Raphael and I stunned at what had transpired while we were away. I can't speak for him, but I could not easily recover from this historic day. So many countries finally side by side. Amazing and wonderful. However, they did not complete the job at hand. Iraq's ruler, Saddam Hussein, was left in place, the man who had started the aggression and indeed was a tyrant toward his own people.

That week I mulled over this situation constantly. I came to the decision that as I was still a young man in my fifties, it wasn't time for me to retire on a beach and dream of writing a great novel. This world was changing every day. Living where I was, I was clearly out of the realm of what was happening in the world. It was time for a change. Three weeks later I moved to Paris and became involved in real life. I admit, there were times that I questioned the sanity of that decision. But it was the right one and I'm pleased I made it.

Addendum

Not many years later, another American President, a son of the one who waged that first incomplete war against Iraq, became head of state in the U.S. He did not go through all the ethical and legal ways he could have employed to avoid yet another war with this country. My mind fills with thoughts of what could and should have taken place.

I haven't been on a fishing boat since 1991. I suppose old memories are with us forever.

✡ ✡ ✡

THE HOUSEBOATS IN FRANCE #1 ... 1992

I knew when we first did it that Americans had previously taken houseboats in France; this was not a novel idea, but now Carol and I could add our names to the list. For three continuous years we motored down three different canals in France. Each year we rented a houseboat for a full week from a company called Locaboat, based in the lovely village of Joigny.

It was a bit odd at first, as people from Locaboat took us to our personal houseboat, appropriately named, "The Buffoon." This was on a Tuesday, October 6, 1992. It would be our home until we returned it on the 13th. There are different sizes: boats for two people, four persons and larger parties. The one we chose was designed more for two people. Though four could have slept aboard, there was only one "bedroom." We also rented two bicycles and they were placed on board. The manager gave us perhaps a twenty minute lesson on how to start, steer, stop and maneuver the vessel through the many locks we would encounter on our voyage. Then, leaving this rather costly boat totally in our far from capable hands, he just departed. Neither of us had any previous experience with a houseboat and now suddenly we were the captain, Carol, and crewman, me!

Even the first closed lock was a major challenge, as Carol steered the houseboat slowly to a grassy bank and I played Errol Flynn, leaping off with a rope in front and one in back to pull us in until the lock reopened. There were a few other boats and we tried to follow the actions of their crews, but of course most knew as little as we did.

Before setting out, Carol and I had gone to a market and stocked up on a few essentials, especially wine and cheese! We had also brought along a cassette players with lots of music and numerous books. Gradually we relaxed. Within a few hours we felt like quite the sailors.

All three of our voyages were distinctly different. This first one was a good starter, as we motored through Bourgogne, Auxerre, and other memorable towns and simple villages. No two days were the same; the scenery changed continuously as we motored along. Occasionally we met a lock manager who had fresh fish, wines, vegetables and various other items to sell. When we felt comfortable we would pedal our bikes with their wicker baskets to small towns and stock up on whatever we needed or fancied. We cooked on board at times, and visited restaurants in charming small villages as well. Their menus never failed to delight, and everything was fresh and sensibly priced. We learned eventually to conquer the fifteen or so locks that we encountered every day. We felt we were in the film "African Queen"; Carol was Ava Gardner and I was Humphrey Bogart.

We love France in October as most tourists have left, the weather is usually mild, with occasionally cool or light showers, but it's pleasant even then. On one particular evening, the canal was quiet and nature was gently changing seasons; the trees and leaves were stunning. With our cassette music from the opera, Edith Piaf or the Eagles singing "Hotel California," nice wines and comfortable dining, albeit the setting perhaps was not exactly elegant, it was impossible not to savor the moment. We looked at the old wooden sign with an arrow on it, used to indicate to boaters which of two canals to take at that time. Unbeknown to us at the time, the wind that had come up and moved the sign the wrong way; of course that was the route we took. The next morning when we went onto the deck, we were stunned. We were no longer on water. In fact, there was no water anywhere. It had all been drained out to the other canal.

After taking a few deep breaths, we made breakfast and just sat and waited. We felt that eventually someone would come by. Alongside us there were grass paths that one could walk on. Our good fortune was that a local farmer on his bike did come along. We waved to him and pointed to the "Locaboat" name written boldly on the side of our vessel. We made the sign with our hands to call them. He understood and made the call. About two hours later there came another surprise. Four men, three of them dressed as divers, arrived. After a brief argument, the manager understood why we had taken the wrong canal. Even so, he was still unhappy and said we would lose our deposit. There was possible damage to the underside of the boat. Also, they now had to open the water into the canal we were on, to allow our vessel to rise. I don't think Moses himself could have done this single-handed. Gradually, the water flowed in. Slowly the divers in their gleaming black wet suits managed to lift the boat and pulled us quite a way, until we were close to the right spot. They dove under to see if there was damage or leaks and gave us the OK signal. In time we received permission to proceed, and after that experience we sailed slowly into the other canal as the water was again switched into it. As I recall, when we were on our way we could only listen to Mozart or Brahms, sip some wine and wonder how all that took place. This new canal was beautiful and we smiled, laughed and sailed onward.

When we returned the houseboat in Joigny, they examined it and said it would need some paint beneath, but they did return part of our deposit. We were wearing jeans and T-shirts and very much wanted to shower and dress normally again. The people at Locaboat recommended a place which turned out to be five star, one of the leading hotels in the world. Dressed as we were, rather unkempt, I had doubts management would even allow us into the lobby. Much to my surprise and happiness, they not only let us in, but rented us a lovely suite. I think that was due more to my American Express card than anything else. We placed our suitcases inside and went to the main outside balcony, where the other guests had congregated for drinks before dinner. We must have looked a sight, like two vagabonds. However, I believe it may have worked for us. It must have created a bit of a stir, causing people to wonder who were these two people, dressed in jeans, but staying at this fabulous hotel? Were they perhaps famous for something? We were observed the entire time we were outside.

We later went to our suite where we showered forever, it seemed. Then we dressed with the proper clothing and went to the restaurant for dinner. There was no way we could know this chef was a master. Placed at a comfortable table, we discussed what foods to dine on for some time with the waiter. My not eating meat posed no problem and we ordered what turned out to be incredible, perhaps the best meal ever. The one item I loved in particular was fresh sea food immersed in the lightest jelly I have ever tasted. The rest of the foods were minimalist and delicious. When a new dish was brought, we tasted it and could only stare at each other. Never before or after have we tasted better sauces and foods.

Afterward we were invited to have special drinks in the establishment's private cellar. One took an elevator down below the earth, walked under the street above it, until one heard music. When we came upon the sound, we discovered it was coming from a three or four piece jazz group. They were playing in a lightly lit, stunning room, whose walls were covered in art. Drinks were served and we relaxed into fabric covered soft chairs. Those people who had seen us only in jeans and T-shirts were now certain that we were important people. We tried not to disillusion them. It was, frankly, quite easy. We only had to remember waking up on a wrong canal with no water under our houseboat, a man on a bicycle, and others in rubber scuba diving suits. Then, by sheer luck, finding this hotel and restaurant. Yes, we were smiling … and I believe we had every reason to do so. This experience could have been a catastrophe. Instead it turned into one of the most enjoyable times we've ever known. There are times we are lucky. This was one of them.

HOUSEBOAT # 2 ... 1993

The thought of taking a houseboat down a French canal seems idyllic, however, it's not always as it seems. I've previously written about 1992 and our first voyage down a canal. The houseboat we chose for our second trip was again meant for two people; while there were sofa beds in the living area, there was only one bedroom, and it slept two. There was also a shower, toilet, and a full if rather cramped kitchen. But for two travelers, with music and books, it was extremely comfortable.

This was 1993, the very next year after our first slightly unnerving experience. We were hooked. Despite the hassle, never had we had such a relaxed and interesting holiday. So we happily signed up again. This time we got the boat in a small village just outside Montpellier, so that we could explore different spots. This was October 16. The ports of call were to be along the west coast of the French Mediterranean: Marseillan, Sète, Aigues-Morte, Saint-Gilles, Beaucaire, the seaside resorts of Palavas, La Grande-Motte, Cap d'Agde (the Naked City – where people dine, walk around town and of course lie on the beach, all in the nude!), and Carnon. Likely just names to you, as they were to us.

There were not many other houseboats afloat, and we didn't mind that one way or another. By this time we both felt that we were in control of our vessel as well as our journey. We didn't know yet what was waiting around the next bend. A group of white wild horses cantered by us on a path just off the lake! They were stunning. Full of energy and strength. Eventually we came to Marseillan, between Étang de Thau and Sète, where the majority of French oysters are grown, on long sticks and nets. It's actually situated out at sea, in an area where we truly were concerned for our houseboat and our own safety. Quite wild and rough.

It happened that outside the port there were some other boats before us. This pleased me, as my thought was to follow them. Instead it was apparent that they had the same ideas about us and in fact, we were to be the leaders of this flotilla! Although neither Carol nor I was pleased, we decided to conquer our fears and go forward. There were signs written in many languages to boaters. The one in English read, "Do not even THINK of coming near our oyster nets."

I can only assume that the other signs were as graphic. Clearly I remember taking the wheel for one of the few times on either of our trips. I had no idea if we were about to approach trouble, but if so, I wanted to be in the frontlines. It was not a macho thing, just that I considered myself capable when faced with physical threats.

I did all I could to avoid the oyster nets and was successful. Had there been a nasty wind or storm, I doubt if I would have been able to win that battle. It was getting late in the day and we decided to moor beside the village of Marseillan, where the oysters were taken, separated and cleaned, before they were transported to Paris or the many villages that specialize in seafood. Most of the other houseboats had the same thought and a number also tied up for the evening.

There were no Americans, just Dutch, Germans, French and a people from a few other countries. We all went together and discovered a charming restaurant with no name. If I recall properly, there must have been about ten to twelve of us. The owner was thrilled and sent a huge plate of oysters to our table as a welcome gift. Stories were told, drinks and laughter rang out and it was one of those evenings that you can't plan for, or ever expect to repeat.

The next morning was filled with glorious sunshine and we went to Aigues-Mortes, a walled city inside a fortress. It's eight hundred years old. The many restaurants and skill of the craftsmen making wooden writing pens by hand keep the fortress alive and vibrant, by attracting numbers of tourists. A delightful place to visit. As we had been dining on only French food, we were longing for something different and hopefully decadent. We found exactly what we wanted at Le Bandido, where we enjoyed a marvelous pizza, and I really mean one of the best ever. These days you can drive there and we certainly recommend it.

As we continued down the canal after our repast, Carol spotted a large boulder on shore about sunset, and pulled over. I grabbed the ropes in front and back, jumped off and hammered them into the earth. She disappeared for a moment, then came out holding something silver. It was an urn. I knew immediately what was to follow and motioned for her to pass by me if she wished. In the urn were some of her mother's ashes. Alone, Carol went to the large rock and quietly spoke. Then she took the ashes and placed them underneath it. To this day I have no idea what she said, as I considered that a very private time between her mother and herself. We left, Carol with a tear in her eye.

The next day was also lovely and we sailed into a charming area with bright green grass, swings and a playground for children. The area was also replete with monuments of soldiers from the village who had long since passed away. But the highlight was the restaurant. Its name: La Bouillabaisse! Our favorite food. No menu was given to us. When I inquired about our choices, I was told that the fishermen were in with the day's catch and the chef was preparing the day's meal. No options, you ate what was caught. So fresh and delicious. We must have spent three hours there enjoying the ambience as well as the food. The locals treated us as if we were neighbors. A marvelous experience.

Afterwards we stocked up on enough provisions to last another day and were fortunate to find a few newspapers in English, even if they were a few days old. I had not realized how hungry I was for news of the outside world. As I scanned the journals from page to page, I had to smile; we had really missed very little in the so called "real" world.

When the voyage was about to end we pulled into shore, discussed how much we had enjoyed it, and concluded, "Lets do it again next year!" We thought we would go onto yet a different French lake and experience more unusual opportunities and scenarios.

We did do it the following year, for what was our last and perhaps most interesting trip.

More on that in the next story. Frankly, I'm ready to go again on a houseboat down a French canal right now.

HOUSEBOAT TRILOGY #3 ... THE END?

In 1992 and 1993 Carol and I so enjoyed our two houseboat trips down French canals that we decided to go for one more. The big one! We suspected it would be difficult, but our previous experiences provided us with the boldness to proceed.

We flew into Paris, where I had a wonderful apartment. She had previously been there. The apartment was on the 21st floor, just a few streets from the Eiffel Tower, and we were able to see it light up its millions of lights in the evening, and hours later, see them slowly diminish into darkness. It was quite large by Parisian standards, and had a marvelous kitchen where I could practice my culinary skills. It was also near marvelous markets, making it easy for me to purchase fresh food every day that I was cooking. As I was a long term tenant, two years, the manager Terry and I had become pals and would often explore the many nooks of Paris that tourists rarely see. I heard that he is now the proud owner of a small hotel and wonderful restaurant on the French-Spanish boarder. It would be a delight to accidentally find it and visit one day.

Carol was there just under a week and we met friends, ate at bistros new even to me, and visited the jazz clubs on the Left Bank. Oysters, seafood plates and a bottle of wine at a comfortable booth near the musicians, and we would be out until two in the morning. Perfect. Other nights if there was rain we would catch a film at one of the many cinemas Paris has to offer. Perhaps mussels and French fries afterwards and always with an umbrella, then walk back to our abode. I do really enjoy L.A., but there is that something extra that the depth of Paris has to offer.

After our delightful days in the city, it was time to prepare for our grand voyage on the last canal. We rented a car and drove to the little village of Carnon to collect the houseboat there. It was similar to the two previous boats and we had no difficulties handling it. We stocked it with a kind of "starter kit" of various foods, wines, a tape player for music and of course books. As we motored, we also knew from our previous trips that the people who man the many locks on canal routes would be pleased to help us replenish our stores with their fresh foods, cheese and various delicacies.

It was on the second night, when I put a piece of soft bread over the stern of the boat that I saw we were being followed. A gorgeous, large white swan was almost alongside. This was after ten in the evening and I was quite surprised. The beautiful bird went for the bread instantly and devoured it, then lifted its head and, if this is possible, our eyes met. I went into the kitchen and found what I hoped were safe and tasty foods for a swan. Carol knew something was happening and quickly joined me. We made it a point not to hurry about or to speak above whispers. Slowly,

we placed the foods into the water. We had chosen well, as our swan friend ate it all. Eventually it approached the side of our craft and we could place certain foods directly into its mouth. After some time, Carol called it a night. But I was fascinated and remained with it. Male or female? No idea. I found a box of crackers it seemed to like and every few minutes I gave it one. In between, it moved close enough that I could actually gently brush it. I had wondered if it might try and take a piece of my hand, but within moments I dismissed that thought. I started to speak to the beautiful creature. I told it who we were, where we came from and where we going and honestly, just quietly rambled on. It seemed that the more I spoke, the more our friend relaxed, and it was now close enough to be onboard. The thought crossed my mind, but then I realized it would be out of its own environment and that was not such a clever idea. But you can't image my surprise when after waking up the next morning and going outside, I saw the swan again, by the side of our houseboat, looking asleep with its lovely neck lying on its body. We fed it and it remained with us for much of the day, only departing when we approached the next lock.
We were fortunate with the weather and proceeded onwards, stopping on occasion to ride our bikes into a village to either have a look-about, perhaps dine at a place that looked interesting, or just visit a small market to stock up, putting our finds into the brown wicker baskets attached to the bikes. As it began to grow late, we decided to go forward another hour or so. That really was a wrong decision, but it turned into a positive ultimately. We had missed some signs and had no idea that we were quickly approaching the city of Strasbourg. No boats were allowed into their canal after 5:00 p.m. It was now almost seven! One does not break the law on land, and there is no difference in the water. As we motored into the city a bright light flashed at us and a siren went off. We understood we were the culprits, but what had we done? Within a few minutes a police boat pulled alongside us and a young man in uniform made it clear that we had done something wrong. He tied his speedboat next to us and boarded our houseboat.

It only took him a minute or so to see we had meant no harm, but rather had just made a human mistake. Carol was sitting having a glass of wine. She stood and poured another and offered it to the policeman. I immediately knew he would either be upset or become a friend of an ordinary couple in a houseboat who had made a mistake they regretted. He took the glass and drank it happily. Then to our surprise he stopped speaking German and French and spoke quite passable English. Carol of course made sure his glass was always full. We spoke of countries, wines and foods. But never politics. He was with us almost a half hour. Then he received another call and told us to follow him. He took us to a very nice area where there were other boats moored for the evening, shook our hands, wished us well, poured himself a last glass of wine and was gone. We could only heave a sigh of relief.

We dressed up a bit and walked into Strasbourg. So old and interesting. A sign by a restaurant called "Le Gruber" stated they had been operating since 1575. Without a reservation we went in, and in time they seated us. I saw they had fresh salmon as a delicacy and we both ordered it. That turned into a major mistake. When it came, there was the salmon, but it was placed between two croissants and literally was covered in cream. It was hard to even see the salmon. Carol was repulsed as much as I was. I explained to the waiter that we simply wanted the salmon and nothing on top of it or below it, and no cream. Baked, grilled or whatever. He was somewhat unpleasant about it and explained that was the way it had been offered for centuries, "Take it or leave it." Our decision was immediate. We got up and walked out. The good news was that we only had to walk a few yards before spying an intriguing Chinese restaurant. The menus were in a window and one was printed in English. We asked the waiter if they could cook simple fresh vegetables or fish, with perhaps the sauces on the side. He understood me perfectly, and promised to bring us what we would enjoy. It was a simple but immaculate place, and the food was delicious. Lady luck was smiling. In the morning we motored near the many stunning international buildings that are located in Strasbourg along the waterfront. The United Nations, major health, banking and numerous others are there. Rather un-European in their modern designs.

Then it was off to the second largest lock in the world. The biggest, we were told, was in Russia. When we approached this one, we knew we were somewhere unique. Many boats of all sizes and countries were already awaiting their turns. The lock felt like a modern miracle. It was massive in design, but yet stunning in looks. You pulled your boat into a canal and moved continuously, until your vessel could go through. Then suddenly you saw your bow headed toward what looked like a drop into an abyss, miles deep. We could have no thought of turning back at this point, even if we'd been allowed to. As we stood by apprehensively, we felt our boat being lifted onto rollers and moved into position. I dare anyone not to feel nervous the first time they approach this lock. Without the mechanical support, I assume a traveler would be doomed, it looked to be such a huge fall.

Finally, amongst all the other boats we found ourselves moving downward quite gently. It felt as if a giant hand were doing it all. Amazed afterwards at how quickly and efficiently we were lowered, thousands of yards, onto yet another canal, Carol and I breathed sighs of relief, had a glass of wine and continued onward.

In all, I consider it a marvelous experience. One time through certainly caused a bit of a fright, but if I am ever confronted by that lock again, I know it will feel simple. I still recall appreciating man's ingenuity in overcoming the forces of nature, once we had cleared the lock.

The softness of the quiet, on a few occasions interrupted by our classical music, was a sheer joy. The wild animals looking from the shores, the meals we cooked on board as well as those we savored in villages, the bike rides to wherever, were moments that I will always cherish as very special.

When our trip was over we flew to a hotel spa in a wonderful place that I hope we will return to one day. Most travelers have heard of Biarritz. Once upon a time it was for the wealthy to congregate and mingle. That era has passed and it's more just a pleasant town now. Although we visited there, we went and stayed a few miles away, in a town called St. Jean de Luz. We checked into our hotel, probably looking as before as if we had just come off a boat. There is a great spa in this hotel, where you work your already tired body for hours, mainly with water treatments. Refreshed, cleaned and spiffy we were now hungry and were advised to try the Basque restaurants just a few streets away. Not expecting much we walked there and were dazzled with all we saw. Perhaps fifty or more restaurants on both sides of two long streets. We spent five days there and perhaps had at least a bite in most of them. We love dining in Italy, but this street is a very close second. We laughed as we exercised hard for a few hours each day at the spa, only to go out later to the street of foods and stuff ourselves. When it came time to fly back to Paris we were sorry on one hand, but certainly knew it was time to make a grateful exit.

The places I've mentioned all still exist and I hope they don't change too much in the future. Delightful towns and villages, people that are genuinely caring and touches of what the world used to be are shrinking in number. Those that never experience them are missing out, but those who do visit them will be rewarded many times over.

This is the finale of this trilogy. Three visits on houseboats on French canals that our minds and hearts will never forget.

2,000'S

Carol and Alon toast to life in Montecatini-Termi

THE DAY I DIED

Last year Carol and I were staying in Lake Lugano, Italy and decided to take a train to Lake Como. George Clooney has a villa there, not that he would invite us in, even if he happened to be there at the time.

We go to Europe two or three times a year and this particular visit was quite a busy one, with stays in Paris and Switzerland. This was in April and it was unusually warm for that time of year. I suppose my age is showing as these visits seem to take a bit out of me after a week or so. In each of the four trips preceding this one I had some health issues. A leg, a shoulder, elbow, just bad luck. Before we left I had a checkup and was told that a few signs on my blood work were only so-so and that we would monitor them from time to time. Some readings were a bit high and others a bit low, but nothing to indicate that I was in any serious difficulty. There was no reason not to go back to Europe.

The visit to Lake Como was only two days before we were due to return to the States. A two hour train ride and a walk beside a lovely lake sounded like an ideal way to complete our stay. We boarded the train about noon and were very comfortable. Carol sat directly across from me. There were other passengers in our particular car, but it wasn't full. We always travel with books and newspapers so our travels would be quite relaxing. Most of the trains in that part of the world are smooth, quiet and a pleasure to travel on. This was to be a major exception.

About an hour into the journey, Carol had just completed something she was reading and looked across at me. She saw that I had turned a grayish white and was unconscious. She screamed my name and tried to awaken me, to no avail. Then for some wondrous inexplicable reason, a man sitting two rows away heard her and immediately came to see what was wrong. He saw my colorless face, took my pulse and said to her that there was NO sign of a pulse, that it looked as if it were too late. However, he pounded my chest as Carol kept calling my name. I can clearly recall something happening, and that I opened my eyes, as if I had just awakened from a nightmare. What I had seen was definitely a white flash.

Other passengers were standing around us and seemed terribly upset. When I realized I was on the floor of the train all I could feel was embarrassment. I saw the concern in everyone's faces and had no idea why I was on my back. The only humorous thing was that I was wearing a very good suede jacket. I just hoped it wasn't damaged.

The train had stopped in the middle of nowhere in particular. No city or town. Suddenly two policemen came through, followed by the ticket collector and a conductor. They did not try and lift or move me. Carol spoke up and said we were just tourists … and then someone who spoke Italian and English acted as her interpreter. They said I should go to a hospital right away. I was not at all keen on that idea. Then the man who had helped me spoke up and I could tell from his accent he was Australian. He just said, "Look here, I'm a medical doctor and just a few minutes ago you were all but dead. There is obviously something very wrong and you may not be as fortunate if there is a recurrence." Carol told him that I was a retired doctor and then he was most insistent that I should know not to leave anything like this to chance. I agreed without hesitation at that point. Also, there was already an ambulance there with two more men. They had a stretcher and carried me out and put my now exhausted body in the back, with Carol sitting next to me. The drivers moved us expertly and fast, and in only a few minutes we were in a small Italian village. My luck held out again, as there was a hospital there that was marvelous. I was placed on a gurney and taken with haste to a room. In the time I was there four doctors examined me, took blood tests, pricked and probed. I've no idea why, but all were women. I never saw a male physician. After over three hours they returned and said that I had a serious iron deficiency and that my platelets were extremely low. I was given two prescriptions, told to have them filled at the pharmacy across the street. They wheeled me out to a waiting taxi, whose driver went with Carol into the pharmacy, which filled the orders in no time. He then drove us back to our hotel in Lake Lugano, about an hour's drive. I took the medication and fell into a deep sleep.

When I awoke I was hungry and felt almost like the whole episode had never transpired. But it had. Carol and I dined in the hotel and talked about what had taken place. Had she not looked up from what she had been reading and seen the condition I was in, or been in the bathroom or dining car … and of all things to have an English speaking medical doctor so close to us in the car, to come to my aid, and if that hospital wasn't so efficient, or the pharmacy had been closed, or was even farther away. Such a small town, they may have had only the one ambulance. Every single one of those details, and I'm sure a few others, had to be there, and perfectly in place. Had even one not worked out … I might never have returned to life. So many intangibles to consider. Humans are strong. However, we can also be oh, so frail.

One sadness is that I have lost and in fact never knew the name of that Australian doctor on the train. Or for that matter the hospital and the doctors there, or ambulance men. There is so much to thank them for. Well, my life for one. Without all of them, I certainly would not be here today.

We're returning April 1st to Europe, Portugal and the Island of Madeira just off the coast. I will get a blood test and full examination within the next two weeks. But last time I was given a clean bill of health. This time I just may give them this to read. Perhaps, and hopefully, I will again be told all is well, and this time they will be right.

The one thing that I don't want to see is that white flash again, as it awakens me to come back to life. Once was enough.

Oh, and by the way, when I was on the floor, what was that white flash, in my mind? I'm an agnostic. But perhaps … I don't know. However, it does make my mind wonder about a very unusual ride on a train … in Italy.

DINING IN MONTECATINI-TERMI, ITALY

In Montecatini-Termi, just above Florence, Italy, Carol and I went to a hotel and spa that was at least 100 years old. The town is famous for its healing waters; believed to cure all one's physical problems. Busloads carry in thousands of people every day who wish to drink the water that flows there. Tables and chairs are set up, and folks praying for miracles drink away. There is a cost for the water, but it's minimal.

We checked into the Grand Hotel, not knowing or frankly caring about the water aspect of the town. Nevertheless, Carol went down almost every morning to try her luck. I visited two or three times in the afternoon. Although the water is supposed to be at its best early, I really don't enjoy mornings.

When checking in at the hotel, I spoke at length with the concierge about dining. I gave him an edict that we would be having dinner out every evening and wanted to go to a different restaurant for each meal. But that one after the other had to be better than the last! The restaurants had to have fish and seafood along with pasta, vegetables, and whatever else was their specialty. We would be drinking the wines only of the region, and we would be taking taxis and not driving ourselves. I intimated that his success would be reflected in the reward he would receive on our departure. He smiled and said that he looked forward to the challenge!

Needless to say, we had seven nights of seeing parts of Tuscany we never would have known about, eating from plates that were perhaps centuries old and overflowing with a mosaic of vegetables and foods from the sea, foods that were not only cooked but also presented to perfection. It seems the concierge called and spoke to all of the chefs and explained the sort of contest we were engaged in. Perhaps we were paparazzi, or magazine food reporters!

Without an iota of exaggeration, we ate the finest homemade pasta, mussels and clams, with calamari so tender it melted in our mouths. Numerous salads, many comprised of herbs from the restaurant's own gardens. A plethora of vegetables that were different from many we'd tasted before, some baked, others roasted, sautéed, or served simply au natural. Each clean and fresh. In some places we were not given a wine list. The restaurateurs chose what we would sip with the various dishes.

Needless to say, we could not have done better. We were awed that each evening the dinners indeed grew more extravagant, not so much in cost or presentation, but in the actual taste of the foods themselves. I've no idea if we were treated above and beyond the restaurateurs' normal fare. We did notice all the native Italians around us eating; perhaps "gourmandizing" is a better word. We considered ourselves simply fortunate that the concierge, or the chefs, or marvelous good fortune, had given us the opportunity to dine on such delicious meals, from family restaurants that are certainly not in Zagat or any high profile books. It was an unforgettable week of incredible dining.

And yes, I certainly did thank the concierge, and left him with a wide smile.

AMAZING!

How did I ever agree to rent a large villa for ten of us in Juan les Pins, France, above Cannes and below Monaco and Italy? I must say, wherever it originated, it was a clever idea, and blossomed into one of the most fun episodes in my life.

To make the villa a reality, I contacted a lady named Sylvia, using the internet. She was a real estate agent, very helpful, and found a perfect house for our group to stay. BUT ... there were conditions: it was costly, and the owner insisted on being paid in cash, French francs at that time.

I called a friendly bank I was dealing with and spoke with the manager, who did not find this very unusual. He set up the transaction, gave us the name and location of the local bank that would be aware of the collection, and said there would be no difficulty. Well, that was HIS interpretation of what would transpire. The reality was quite different.

A few weeks later Carol, Sylvia and I arrived at the rather small bank in Sylvia's car. There was a line, of perhaps ten or so people, and I was concerned. This was to be a rather sizeable amount of money, but there was no guard or protective force there at all. They had the ten thousand dollars, but in the small bills that were French francs, it was a lot of paper.

It was stacked up, so that everyone could view it. I was not even offered a bag to place it in. I reached for the pile, took it and stuffed it into my underwear. Not comfortable but I hoped much safer. All this in a bank, no less.

Sylvia and Carol were chatting amiably in her car and had no idea what had taken place. I suppose I acted like a bank robber when I leapt into the car and almost screamed, "Let's go!"

But Sylvia said she had a plumber going to her house and had to be there to let him in. No problem, we replied. When we went into her home, I asked for a bag and she gave me one from a market. Then I asked where the bathroom was and went into it. In the bathroom I dropped my pants, and underwear and cash flew out all over the floor. This was the exact moment that the plumber opened the door and walked in! I have no idea what went through his mind as he raced out of the house. Sylvia ran after him, as he had not repaired whatever he was there for. Perhaps a minute later Carol and Sylvia came into the bathroom and saw me in my underwear, and the floor littered with French francs. The looks on their faces were priceless, but no doubt I wore one as well. The plumber had driven away and I am certain he had a story to tell his friends for many a year.

After the girls heard what the full story was, they had a great laugh. I've never learned if Sylvia got that plumber to return.

With the cash now in a bag, we drove to the villa and proceeded to rent it for two weeks. The husband was, and perhaps still is, the president of the largest insurance company in France. Why he rented out this huge wonderful home every summer, I still cannot figure out. The one answer is that we paid in cash, no checks, and he actually turned his back to us when the money was given to his wife. I suppose that way he could tell the tax man that he never took anything from anyone.

When the transaction was completed, they brought out wines and light snacks and we all sat around like old friends. His wife did take the money to count in a different room. I had no intention of telling her where it had been.

My brother, his son and a friend, his daughter also with a friend, our twin daughters and a long lost cousin with his son Aaron, all rented cars and somehow found their way to the villa. Very surprisingly, they worked out the bedroom situation among themselves; I was not about to play referee, so this was a blessing. I'm sure it was not exactly a hardship. There were six or seven bedrooms.

We went to the markets and bought what we needed, and cooked in every other evening, sampling local restaurants on the alternate nights. There was an Olympic size swimming pool where I spent most of my time, and a wonderful cassette system that could be heard in every room. I had brought books and knew where most of my time would be spent. The others took a train into Italy, went to the beach or shared a bottle of wine at the house with me. It was idyllic.

One evening Rick, Carol's cousin, wanted to go to a club in Cannes. He practically begged me to join him as he was concerned over a number of things. In the South of France all the so-called "action" happens close to midnight. The younger group was already out, Carol was asleep, and my brother Steve was watching CNN on television. Thus I relented, and Rick and I drove to the "hot spot," Cannes. Rick has a thick mustache and looks like Omar Sharif, and I suppose that the doorman thought he had that sort of money, which was a wrong supposition. Nevertheless we were admitted, and I could only smile at fat men and skinny girls attempting to dance with strobe lights and loud music blaring. As I recall I had no conversation with anyone.

Rick quickly vanished although I told him we definitely were going back home before 2:00 a.m. Much to my surprise, he came back to me at about 1:30 with two Swedish girls he wanted to take back with us. I reminded him that I was married to his cousin who very likely would not appreciate waking up to a blond Swedish girl and me. He grasped the situation and although she spoke no French or Swedish, one girl disappeared and the other came with us. She would share the room with Rick and Aaron and his son. Aaron changed rooms the next day and we seldom saw Rick or her afterwards. In the morning Carol asked if there was anything new to report and I said perhaps there was. Sometime that afternoon Rick came to lunch with his new fiancée and you can only imagine the looks on everyone's faces. The only problem was they then looked at me as a culprit and part of this conspiracy. I know he proposed marriage to her and she accepted. They actually continued a long distance telephone and letter writing relationship for some months afterwards. They did not see each other again, of course. I never even learned her name.

Rick's still single, in his fifties, and every so often mentions going to Sweden to find her. Dreams and fantasies.

Carol? Well, we never discussed it, and I'm certain we never will.

ON THE ROAD TO LOS ANGELES ... AND BACK AGAIN

Prior to my maiden stay in Los Angeles, Joey Farsina and I left Miami in a car that we were paid to drive to New York. The car was a new Lincoln, and we were given gas money and a few dollars more for incidentals. We were both in our teens and hardly negotiated for more. From New York we took the train to Philadelphia, where we bought an old Buick. Instead of returning to Miami, we decided to follow our dream and go to California.

We had some fun experiences on the way, and what should have been only two days turned into almost a week. However, no complaints. We found ourselves in Arizona, New Mexico, Nevada. We were so lost. And enjoyed almost every minute.

When we finally arrived in Los Angeles, it seemed like just another big city. Wrong. Very wrong. We found a place on Argyle

Street in the center of Hollywood, with a swimming pool no less. No question. We took it.

In the next few months Joey found a girl as overweight as he was and they became a couple. I had a brief affair with a lovely woman of 63, who played the violin in the Los Angeles Symphony Orchestra. We actually learned quite a bit from each other. Very interesting. Somehow, I discovered the lower half of a house that was available for a reasonable price if the lady owner OK'd it. She did, and I discovered it had been Charley Chaplin's first Hollywood abode. Amazing!

It was a marvelous period. I loved the beach at Malibu, the mountains in Big Bear and Lake Arrowhead. The desert in Palm Springs took only two hours to reach. Whatever one wanted was just a short drive away.

Since that magical time, I've lived in a number of countries, cities, even villages. But in the end I have come back to L.A. I'm about 70 years of age as I write this piece. Not elderly by any means, but now I have to put other factors into this equation of ideal places to live ... good weather, closeness to my brother and his and Carol's kids, and our grandkids. It's not been a difficult decision. So many places I've enjoyed and hope to revisit. However, Los Angeles offers so much. Surely, there is nowhere that is perfect. But for me, this is home.

HOUSES IN WHICH I'VE LIVED

I guess you could call my first "house" Saint Luke's Hospital, the place in Philadelphia where I was born on August 5th, 1939.

At the time, our family lived with my mother's parents, Max and Rose Josephson, in their row house on Delancey Street. As I recall, it was a very popular thoroughfare. My father managed to buy us our own place about a year later on Pine Street, a short walk away. We were there for about twelve years. Brother Steve was born three years after me, on February 16th, 1943. We were a happy group and remained that way always.

I was a handful, though, always getting into scrapes and never regretting any of them. I had a buddy named Cookie. Nationality unknown and in those days, no one cared. We couldn't beat each other, so we joined forces. We were about 10 years old and life was good. Then I discovered our family was moving to a place called Overbrook Park. The teachers were ecstatic. I thought Cookie would be pleased, as he was now Number 0ne and no longer just a partner. Instead he was saddened, and I lost the first real pal I ever knew. We were never in touch again, but I heard he joined the army and met his fate in Korea. Sad if true.

Next Dad bought a business in Wynnefield, just a few streets off the Main Line. We moved again, to live in the apartment above the store. Steve and I shared a large room with single beds, and were comfortable.

Some five years later, when Dad was told he had a bad valve in his heart, he was also told he would live longer in a warmer climate. So we moved to Miami Beach for the heat and humidity. Life certainly changed. For example, during the time we were there, I spent two summers in Cuba, which gave me a taste of what other places could be like. When Dad died things changed again. We stayed in the house, and I had to grow up rather fast

A few years after Dad died, we moved back to Philadelphia, where we had family and friends. But I had acted at the University of Miami and an agent who was there requested I visit him when next in New York. A place I had never been. A few months later I was a resident at 65 Riverside Drive, in Manhattan. It was an interesting year, bringing new friends, acting on stage, modeling. In general, New York broadened my worldview.

When the year was up I returned to Philly and unintentionally got into a vicious vending machine war with a Mafia stooge named Jake. A bull of a man, he made a call to Del Coleman, the largest manufacturer of vending equipment in America. Del in turn called me, making me an offer I couldn't refuse. I flew to Chicago and never looked back. For a youngster just out of his teens, I was moving in ways that were indeed unusual, just as Dad had recommended. Del paid my way to Europe, including all expenses, and shipped his used equipment there for me to market. Almost a million dollars worth of machines, which today would be worth possibly worth 5 million. I went to country after country, many I had never heard of. But I sold every single unit and earned a 15% commission for each sale. I didn't leave Europe for years. More about the vending machine episode in my life on page 107.

At the same time as I was selling vending equipment and based in London, I decided to pursue a medical degree. Guy's Hospital accepted me as a night class student. In business during the day and in class at night, I was a busy young man. I lived in an area called Hampstead Garden Suburb, with Jane and Robin. Both intelligent, lovely girls. Plus, we shared the one king sized waterbed, which seemed to make a 24 hour day much longer. Eventually, Robin and I attended Jane's wedding. She married a man 20 years older, who truly loved her. Robin got engaged to an English photographer. Rather than fly, she took a ship back to America to tell her family. On the ship she met another fellow, fell in love and married him instead. I never saw her again. Life and its games.

A couple of years after I had sold out all of my vending equipment, I got the idea that waterbeds, which were big sellers in the U.S., would be attractive to people in England, and other countries as well. I found living quarters that had attractive retail space on the ground level, in the center of Hampstead at Canfield Gardens, and moved to the new location. After two years there my accountant advised me to buy a home, not rent any longer. I purchased a rather charming place in Finchley. Three floors. Rather narrow, but odd and unique, with a nice garden in the back. Two years later I sold it for a pleasant profit and bought a building off of Bond Street. Downstairs were my offices and the upstairs flat was my home. Not great, but it reduced my driving time to zero and it sufficed for almost three years before I sold it. I also rented a place by the week off Silom road in Bangkok, as I had a factory there. London to Thailand every month for over two years was a bit too much, but I managed it for a while.

Then I bought a town house at 18 Wheatley Street in London, and basically gutted it to bring it up to what I really wanted in a home — complete with spiral staircases and the latest in air conditioning and heat. The place was almost 100 years old and nothing new had been done to it in all that time. I was unaware that I needed to get the local board's planning permission to carry out those improvements. When they discovered what I had done, they wanted me to tear everything out and replace all the ancient radiators and old kitchen equipment, stove, refrigerator, power points that were there previously. I refused and stated I was prepared to go to court. They sent two people who examined everything and refused to say a word to me. But two days later I had a note placed under my door stating I now had full permission to carry out my "intended" improvements. A few years later I sold the house to an Australian lady who not only bought it at my very inflated asking price, but gave me a check at a local bank to cash immediately. She didn't want anyone to come in and top her offer. A few years ago, Carol and I were walking by the place and met her. She was so pleased to tell me she had just resold it, for five times what she paid. Good for her!

Next I bought land and had a house built to my specifications in Portugal, in the area called The Algarve. It was idyllic, but after four years I was becoming bored. I sold it and moved to Paris, which was wonderful to live in. The apartment I found was on the 21st floor of a building very close to the Eiffel tower. I could clearly see the lights go on and off at night.

Then I met Carol on that visit to Los Angeles. Life changed. Eventually no more Paris, but Ventura Boulevard in Woodland Hills until the earthquake. Now it's Wilshire Boulevard, between Westwood and Beverly Hills. I'm very comfortable here and with frequent visits to Europe I believe this is where I'll stay.

* * *

THOUGHTS POLITICAL ...
GROWING UP IN POLITICS

Though there is no special moment in politics that stands out as truly important when I was just a young lad, I do recall that my parents and their friends were lifelong Democrats. I did hear one man speak who was running for president in the 1950's, and was captivated by his language; he was so intelligent. I came to understand that very quality is what held him back; the average American really could not understand him or warm up to him. Pure lack of education at work in our country.

Other elections followed, and frankly whatever Mom and Dad said was good enough for me. I was young and none of my friends took much notice of these various men running for election. I can recall names thrown about like Dewey, Truman, Eisenhower and the colorful mayors from Chicago, New York and Philadelphia. It was John Kennedy that I truly took notice of, especially after the Cuban Missile Crisis. I remember Khrushchev going to the United Nations and taking a shoe off, so that he could use it as hammer to bang when he was unhappy. And Fidel Castro going in with a pistol, either to impress or for self protection. Mostly I looked at the famed UN as a group of well paid fat cats, trying to stay awake.

Funny side story ... In later years, one afternoon in about 1992, a friend, Michael Cole, Carol and I were at the UN for lunch. While Michael and I discussed business Carol read a newspaper. Unfortunately, she held the paper a bit too close to the lit candle on our table, and it caught fire! The staff quickly put it out, and we managed to convince them that the fire was an accident, and it was not our intention to burn down the United Nations building. We were permitted to remain for lunch. I don't think we ever returned.

Another political recollection ... I was in the Hollywood Hills, with an aspiring actress, on a sofa with the TV on, and wonderful music moving us onward. Then came the interruption — the President had been shot in Dallas. We moved to the floor in front of the TV, fixated on the screen. Numb with disbelief, we followed every visual they showed, and shed tears of enormous sadness and loss.

Certainly the assassination of Kennedy was not sudden, although it seemed so. A place called Viet Nam and its terror also gained notoriety. I had no idea why we were involved in a domestic, one country dispute. Ordinarily, whichever administration was in place, I was behind them 100%. This action though, created a unique puzzle. There were protestors from both sides and I tried to listen seriously to them all. Who was right and who not? My answer came as a result of a letter stating that I was now allowed to proceed to England, to follow through with various vocations and ideas I had held for a few years now.

Once living in London, I found myself following not only English politics, but also worldwide political events and opinions. I was traveling extensively, eventually to fifty-five countries, and wanted to be erudite in everything about the places I was flying into. Politics were second on my list, after correct manners. There were medical colleagues who on occasion got into trouble and had problems. They were mostly pompous Englishmen who could not be bothered with the customs of other countries. I was completely the opposite and even tried to learn a few sentences of each language. Consequently, I was frequently invited to the offices and even the homes of those locals who were held in esteem. Under religion, my passports all said that I was C of E. The few times I was asked, I said, it meant Church of Ecology. I am certain most knew my religion, but I was speaking about health care, not weapons or war. As I look back on it, I believe I visited every Arab and Moslem country. Yes, there were a few unpleasant moments, but my hosts stood up for me.

When in England, if someone was overly critical about the United States, I always asked the same question, "When was the last time you were in the States?" The answer was almost always, "I never was there." At that point I would give them a look, and say that that the conversation was over. I refused to discuss my country with someone who had literally no experience there, and who was just voicing a secondhand opinion. That doesn't work.

I met Mrs. Thatcher on one business occasion. Cold but exceptionally bright. I cannot say I liked her, but I certainly respected her. I did invite Princess Margaret for a drink at Errol's Court Hall, where there was a medical exhibition. It was, as the English say, "cheeky" of me. But she accepted! And with her bodyguard behind us we each had a glass of wine. She was there as a member of the Royal family. I was there to make a living. My recollection is that we may actually have had a second glass, as we were laughing about something nonsensical and I had forgotten that I was a mere commoner!

When In China or Taiwan I used two passports so as not to offend people of one or the other country. In Japan, Malaysia, Indonesia or any of the Far East countries, I learned their religion, history, political beliefs and leader's name before going. My being a vegetarian actually helped in many instances. The groups I traveled with had to eat the monkey brains, bears paws and sheep's eyes. I dined on vegetables and fruits.

Everyone in any country I ever visited liked and appreciated Bill Clinton. When the Lewinsky situation took place, NO ONE ANYWHERE could understand why America was so hard on him. After all, he was excellent in his position as President, and the country was prospering greatly. His situation with Monica was between him and his wife.
He was castigated to a degree that now he is actually looked upon more fondly abroad than he is in America. But his enemies in the

U.S. got their pound of flesh. Actually, these ill-minded buffoons and we, the people, received much more than Clinton's pound of flesh. We also got the despicable cabal of Bush, Cheney and Rumsfeld …

Indeed, *Well, Ollie, this is a fine mess you got me into.*

POLITICS ... NEWS OF TODAY
Written in 2008

There are perhaps thousands of books on this ever-changing subject. I only have a few pages to contribute, but I will share some of my thoughts with you. I will not go back to Abraham Lincoln or Winston Churchill, or any of those who ruled many years ago. This is about today. Now. Some of what I write here could change quickly. Frankly, I hope so.

I believe that the United States is ruled by two uncaring, deceitful men, within a small cabal of similar minded people. History, I am certain, will prove that George W. Bush and Richard (Dick) Cheney have governed this land as if it were their own private domain. Their reign has been a true catastrophe for this nation, its citizens and millions of others around the globe. Although Americans vote for their leaders, from the time of their first term there have been doubts that these two were legally elected. Nonetheless, they are the President and Vice President, and will remain so until November.

Fortunately, Donald Rumsfeld resigned, and now we see Bush and Cheney's advisor, Carl Rove, under indictment. However, even though they are now lame ducks, Bush and Cheney are still, as far as I am concerned, ignoring the wishes of the people to further their own agendas. They concocted a war with a country that meant us no harm. Yes, the people of Iraq had been ruled by a tyrant, but we are not the policemen of the world. Iraqis were not prepared militarily to start a war of their own against us, and could not have done so for many years, even if they wanted to. But by igniting and continuing this ill-founded war, and committing other highly questionable acts, Bush and Cheney have increased their personal pots of gold many times over. At the same time, more U.S. citizens — as well as people in other countries — join the tens of millions who have been driven to live under dire conditions.

Earlier, when Iraq invaded Kuwait in 1991, our country in its self-appointed role as the world's police, led the charge to defeat Saddam Hussein's soldiers, and succeeded quickly, with the help of dozens of Allies who fought alongside us. This time around, the Bush-Cheney conspirators could only cajole a few others into joining their reprehensible plan. One was the United Kingdom and its Prime Minister Tony Blair. At the time of this writing, well over 4,000 American men and women have been killed in this second war against Iraq, plus over a thousand more of the English and other troops that joined with us. These soldiers went to war in Iraq believing the lies fed to them by the American, and British, leaders. Today Mr. Blair is gone, but not with the well wishes of the people of England whom he served so well, up until the run-up to this second Iraq invasion. Leaders of Germany, France, Italy, and other countries have also been replaced. It's too early to know if this injection of "new leadership" will make a difference, but certainly it can't do much worse. Or so we hope.

There is another side of this gloomy story in the U.S. I have a group of friends who will vote for Senator McCain, or ANY Republican who might be running for President. Politics is a subject these friends studiously avoid in my presence. These are men in their 60's, reasonably successful financially. Not wealthy, but certainly comfortable. Some married, others no longer. Their philosophy is that for them life is not bad. They may have to cut back in a few areas, but, under Republican rule they're doing O.K. When I say to them that there are others in the world, indeed in our own city, who need assistance, they shrug and say, "That's for the younger people to deal with. At this stage of life, I have myself to be concerned about."

This attitude is pervasive not only among people I know in Los Angeles. Friends and acquaintances in Miami, a number of folks I know in the Northeast and in other parts of the West besides L.A. also voice this point of view. When I say to them it does not have to be only about money, perhaps they could help with their time, I'm told, "Time is money," and, "People have to look after themselves." I mention this, as now that we know who the candidates will be in November, there is at the moment no slam dunk for either one.

Certainly Senator McCain should be better equipped, with his background, to deal with terrorism at this moment. However, I think that if he is elected, for the most part he will follow the present administration's views and policies. That's a road map for disaster. Senator Obama, I would hope, will gather up the best minds available to advise him on how to deal with any unpleasant situations that arise.

McCain will be 73 and has a history of cancer and health problems. His Vice President will need to be someone who can lead if he falls ill. Senator Obama, the first African American to be chosen to run for the office of president, does not have the experience of others, and has in the past had some dubious friends, but he is extremely bright and in a short period will learn whom he should trust. Sadly, he has already received death threats. Thus, he also must also choose a Vice President carefully. Lyndon Johnson served out President Kennedy's term after he was assassinated, but decided he could not run again as he did not have the confidence of the people, and would no doubt fail in an election. I believe that now, more than ever before, the Vice Presidency is vital to the well being of this nation.

I've spent some time looking through various newspapers and I am somewhat frustrated by all the many problems there are in America, and certainly the entire planet, global warming being just one of a whole panoply. In my adult lifetime, there has never been a period I can recall during which so much pain has been visited on so many people worldwide. No continent or people is being spared.

Leaders will need to stop padding their personal bank accounts and make sure their citizens' lives are improving. Many leaders as well as members of the public complain about gasoline prices. However, those in Europe have dealt with this problem for years, and of course today the euro and pound sterling are far more valuable than the lowly dollar. Arab oil is being poured into its barrels at the highest price ever, and our money is being poured into the producers' bank accounts as never before. The good news is that this will not last. Automobile and aircraft manufacturers are finally realizing that they will no longer be able to sell the big gas guzzlers that have brought them so much profit in previous years. Research and development funds are being aimed at supplanting everyone's dependence on oil with sources of energy that are much less costly, but just as effective.

Cancer, AIDS, and so many other sicknesses are still ravaging us throughout the world. Education levels in America are far below those in a number of other countries. But it is the American tax payer who is funding military in Iraq, Afghanistan, Korea, Germany, Japan, Panama and at least a half dozen other countries! WHY? Have we finally lowered ourselves to become mercenaries to friendly dictators?

Valerie Plame risked her life in many situations, something no one in the Bush administration ever did. But some insidious political being decided to let it out that she was an American spy, working under cover. Her husband was sent to the country called Niger, a poor state in terms of money and power. He was told there was a substance there, enriched uranium — the stuff of bombs — that actually never was on Nigerian soil.

So many questions we have, and they have never been answered. Hide the facts; that's been this administration's nom de guerre.

I'm enclosing real headlines from both the *London Financial Times* and the *Los Angeles Times*, discussing the realities of today. Items that state oil just jumped $10 a barrel, the most in history on any given day; that European and Asian banks' have announced their interest rates may have to be increased —if this comes to pass, forget holidays there, and look to increased prices on their goods here. A senior economic analyst has predicted that oil will go from $133 dollars a barrel now, to $150 dollars by July 4th. Bush has admitted he never reads newspapers or watches the news on television. Cheney never admits anything …

Bits and pieces: Brazil has just raised its oil rates. Malaysia suddenly raised the price of oil to consumers, a 40% hike in one day! The once wealthy country of Rhodesia, now known as Zimbabwe, is undergoing mass hunger. People in more than half of Africa and much of the Middle East are suffering the same fate. Our two top American Air Force leaders were fired last week. It seems that an Air Force jet with five nuclear bombs on board flew across the United States and NO ONE KNEW they were on board. Had that plane gone down … the damage is incalculable. We also accidently shipped a box of nuclear equipment to Taiwan. It was discovered before the Taiwanese took possession of it. Had this deadly material not been found in time, who knows what damage it could have wrought?

If this essay sounds frightening thus far, let us not forget Israel and Iran. Or is it the USA, Israel and Iran? If all the economic, political, religious, social and other tensions are really going to result in an expanded war, EVERYONE will suffer! Although almost everything I read states that Bush and Cheney want further warfare to take place for a reason that is for pure ego, as well as more money in their own and friends' pockets, we must hope that clearer heads prevail. I know that Obama does NOT want war. I am unsure of the McClain position. His comments on Iraq trouble me, those about winning there, not even speaking with our enemies, or potential ones, prior to escalating our invasions and warfare. But even if he had a conversation with these people, it would not turn McClain into a Chamberlain.

I will conclude with this piece of bitterness … it was announced on Friday that over one million homes are being foreclosed on in America. Never in history have we reached these numbers. Not even during the Great Depression. Is help on the way? No, certainly not, at least not until next year. At which time a new, and I pray, honest and caring administration can begin the exhausting cleanup of the mess that will confront them.

I saw my two grandsons the other evening. Just a few months old. I've no idea what sort of America or world they will enter as they become adults. At this time in history, it is not a great legacy we are leaving.

THOUGHTS PERSONAL: THE CYCLE OF LIFE
Maintaining Health of Mind and Body

This piece is an outline of my history of physical and mental health, and also contains insights into my philosophy of life. Drafted as an early exercise in my memoir writing class, it's included here for any help it may give my family and friends in understanding the basic life practices I feel have been instrumental in my life, a life relatively free of physical ailments, one that prizes adventure, romance and, fortunately, has met with success in different professional realms. If this helps just a few people in their own lives, I will be pleased.

* * *

I believe that my health and body, even with numerous accidents and certain potentially hazardous events, have been a positive in my life. You will find practices I believe contribute to one's health that some physicians will not agree with, such as diet. My argument is: it's difficult to debate with success. I've lived longer than any male in my family has.

The second question we considered in our class concerns our body image now vs. when we were teenagers. This strikes me as rather odd. Very few individuals over 60 can make the statement that their body image is similar now to when it was when they were in their adolescence. Myself included.

Where does my viewpoint on maintaining good health come from? Observing those in both poor and good health, and emulating as best possible those living well. I also feel education is important, and I constantly keep abreast of mind and body health research. Key to my good diet principles: other than drinking perhaps a bit of too much good wine, nothing negative do I ever consume.

I have always been a physical person and there is no question that this has played a large part in my sexual identity. A healthy body and mind certainly improve that area of life. It's an activity I've always enjoyed. I started quite young and still enjoy it!

As a baby and child, I was very fortunate, without any unusual difficulties. The older one becomes, the more real life and difficult situations arise, and the more things can become unusual and complicated. But in my case, I wouldn't call them difficulties, as I feel I have been extremely fortunate all my life. Whenever an event or situation emerged that could have devastated me, on the contrary it seems to have brought me to a new place that was better than any I could have planned.

A resounding YES, there have been numerous accidents in my life: Serious car accidents that I was extremely lucky to have lived through. Not many people can say they were in a taxi in Egypt when a truck loaded with cement lost control and crashed into them. Or in a car at night in Portugal that slammed into another, black, that was parked in the middle of a narrow road with no lighting anywhere. Or shot in the arm by a stray bullet in New York. Then there was that time when I lost my vision one morning in London and was hit by a car, which proved to be a godsend, as the doctors found I had a brain tumor. And the time I was on a plane in Lisbon flying to see my brother in Los Angeles, who just had a heart attack, when on takeoff a bomb exploded in the luggage hold. I could relate another dozen episodes, but I think you get the picture. Life has indeed been filled with events! By the way, I was never the driver in any of those accidents.

I've had operations on far too many parts of my anatomy: both shoulders, femur, hands, thumbs, lower back, brain, etc. But the only ones that I suffer from today are my knees, each operated on twice. I'm told that I'm a prime candidate for knee replacement, but will hold off until I have no choice. I'm considering the surgery due to the fact that walking, jogging and gym work are difficult, and oftentimes painful. However, I still try to do them on a semi-regular basis.

I had marvelous parents who always encouraged physical activity and plenty of sports. Thus I don't even recall any unusual amount of time spent on illnesses in my youth.

I was a normally developed child. Although perhaps, an overachiever. I have been doing very well in most aspects of life, and had to struggle with only a few others. I never minded taking certain chances that friends elected to avoid. I moved to Los Angeles and then to Europe and usually friends asked to join me. But when "moving day" arrived, I always had to go it alone. Consequently, I felt sincerely secure in my self image.

As a child I was a confident youngster, with lots of friends, male and female. I was most interested in athletics, and appreciated the value of school and education. I was told I was attractive and performed in the theater and on TV That was enjoyable, kept me feeling youthful, and I think of it as "fun time." But there came a period that I realized that I was ready to put that era behind me, and moved my life forward. As this regards health, I should mention that I have visited a gym or a field almost every day. Stress is an area I always dealt with well as it arose. I believe this ability and inclination stems from self-confidence. But as I age, I find that it's becoming harder to manage. I am working on various areas of my life so that I can overcome stress again on an ongoing basis, and hold its effects at bay. Physically I certainly cannot perform as well I did in my youth, and mentally I'm not as sharp or as quick as I used to be. It will not be long before I reach 70 and the thought of an even older age concerns me. But I know people in their 80's and 90's who are still living a quality life, and that's my goal as well.

What have I done to hurt myself? Perhaps I took a few too many chances in life. Traveled in some dangerous places and took risks that as I look back on now, seem too extreme. And perhaps my love of fine wine led to a compromise of my liver.

To help myself? First and foremost, my diet. I never smoked. I haven't touched a piece of meat in about 45 years. If it walks on land or flies I never eat it. Food from the sea, I will. I've tasted coffee and don't care for it, so never drink it. No caffeine at all. So a good diet and exercise, they're my ticket.

If I could change any parts of my body, it would be my knees and eyesight; I'd like to be able to see without glasses. But I can still get around and read, so I'm not complaining. I recognize that I have some senior anxiety, which I am aware of and doing my best to deal with.

In sum, I never, ever cheat on my diet. I exercise as much as I can. I'm there for my family and loved ones. And I do unto others as I would have them do unto me. I try to treat each day as a blessing!

WHEN MY TEACHER ASKED US TO THINK ABOUT DEATH

I don't recall ever thinking about death as a young child. I never had a pet until I was much older, and I was quickly over their deaths. My parents set the tone regarding handling death in our home. We needed to act like adults at funerals, even when we were young. We never "suffered" from a family member's passing. It was more or less taken for granted that when you get old or just very sick, death follows. No trauma or drama.

As I've gone through life since that time, while I have always tended to take my parents' view that life is ephemeral, and that death is a natural progression, nonetheless many passings have affected me, my parents' being the most significant and difficult. My father Leon (whom everyone called Lee) was only 44, and it was his imminent departure that first brought death to my consciousness.

We spoke about his coming death, with him explaining things clearly. Then, early one evening, he wasn't feeling so hot, and went to the hospital. One of his four valves had collapsed. He passed away the next morning. Today they would have replaced the valve, he'd have been out the same day and we'd have gone to a ball game.

As you can tell from my stories at the beginning of this book, I often think of my parents, and my mother's grandparents, too, with great affection. None of the passings were welcomed. And I do grieve at times about their having died, but then I accept the fact that they are gone; there is nothing I can do about it.

PASSINGS OF OTHER PEOPLE CLOSE OR JUST HELD IN HIGH REGARD

I have also been affected by the deaths of people such as Ernest Hemingway, President Kennedy, Joe Louis, Golda Meir, and good friends and family. When I read or hear of a person's passing that I had respect for, I think of them for an extended period of time. However, I'm able to resolve those issues within my own mind fairly quickly. I come to the realization that I can't reverse what has happened, and I hope they're in a better place, if there is such a place.

ABOUT DEATH IN WAR, AND OTHER SENSELESS DEATHS

Many wartime deaths have troubled me. When you see a bunch of bodies that have been blown up in war, that's not just a tragedy.

That's sickening. Or you read about these sick kids in the U.S. who are shooting other kids, it's beyond tragedy.

I understand people's hatreds, but why their leaders have to get into wars makes no sense to me at all.

To my knowledge, I have not been responsible for any deaths.

THINKING AHEAD

My idea or thought of death is that it will take place eventually for everyone. In my own case, I hope that neither I, nor my family or friends will suffer needlessly during my time.

I obviously hope I can pass in my sleep without pain. I am not ready for many reasons to depart, but I am prepared to accept it. Although I do want a nice funeral and gravesite burial, I hope that it will not be a hurtful experience for my family, and more like a celebration about the fact that I lived a reasonably long and eventful life. Very little time here was wasted and I know that I did do well for many people. I have no one to apologize to, no major regrets, as I feel I gave back to life, easily as much as I've taken from it. The best part of it is, that although I had quite an interesting and active life in my youth, this ending will be with a smile on my face. I'm asking that the words, "Another day in Paradise" be written on my tombstone.

LIFE SHAPERS
The Effect Of Art In My Life

I'm pleased to say that art has influenced my life since I was a very young man. My mother and father loved music. My dad could sing beautifully and there was even a record made of him. He was friendly with Eddie Fisher during Fisher's heyday and they would croon together on occasion. My mother was the consummate reader. Always with a book. I believe she was a significant influence on my love of books and literature. She did have one rule. If a book was unable to hold her attention after 20 pages or so, she would stop reading it and go on to another. I still recall the first novel I read, *The Amboy Dukes*. It was written by Irving Shulman. It had some four letter words in it so I never read it around her! A teacher later gave me books by Mark Twain, Hemingway, Somerset Maugham, James Joyce and many other serious writers of that day and earlier periods. English, Greek, American it didn't matter. I was hooked. *Lawrence of Arabia* took forever to finish, but I was determined and did. I could write pages about books. They are extremely important to me.

I always enjoyed good films. However, I don't know anyone who has walked out on more than I have. One oddity was that even as a youngster I went into the lobby when Walt Disney comics came on before the film. I found them inane and to sit and watch a mouse or some other animated character simply left me cold. And this was when I was just a youngster of 8 or 9. I've thought about that, but have never understood why. However, when the news reels came on, I was glued to my seat. I was fortunate to see films that were fascinating. The Director Costa Gravis made *Z.* Then I *saw The Battle of Algiers,* in which I thought I was seeing a news reel, but it was just great film making. *Some like it Hot, Casablanca, Rear Window ...* numerous others I so enjoyed. When I moved to Europe I saw dozens of foreign films and was seldom disappointed. This is not to intimate that there are not good films made today; there certainly are. I'm just taking a trip down Memory Lane.

The year I spent in New York, I made great friends with two very much older (60's at least) Shakespearean actors, Norman Roland

and his wife. We were chalk and cheese different from each other, but for some reason they sort of adopted me. Perhaps as a project. They took me to see *My Fair Lady, Westside Story*, many classical plays and a host of others. All with original casts. Live drama was an art form that mesmerized me. Since that time, I've so enjoyed the theater, and it certainly has made an impact on my life.

Music is a medium that usually makes me smile. If you meander through our collection you will find everything from jazz, like Chet Baker and Ella, to genres and performers far too numerous to mention. Pop! One weak moment I actually was watching a TV show that advertised "Oldies but Goodies" music on numerous disks from the 60's and 70's. I bought the collection. They still bring back good memories. The classics, Vivaldi, Brahms, Mozart, and even some country and western. I never tire of hearing French (Aznavour, Piaf), Portuguese Fado, Italian, from Mario Lanza to Bocelli or Pavarotti. I had almost a thousand vinyl 78 speed records, acquired from a restaurant in Antwerp, Belgium, that was going out of business. I kept them in our storage unit. But then it rained for two days. The deluge came through the ceiling, warping and destroying every single disk. C'est la vie. I think I heard them all, or at least the ones I felt were meaningful.

In my London town house I was displeased with my dining room table and chairs. They were similar to everyone's, and I thought they were boring. A few months later, in December, 1991, my brother Steve and I went to Bangkok, Thailand. I saw a magazine article that had a story of a furniture factory in Chang Mai that made furniture to your design. I remember it was early afternoon on a very hot day when we met with the lady owner. She was kind and receptive. In order to help me make my selection, the lady owner had her staff begin to bring out different dining chairs and tables for me to view. As the collection was clearly extensive, Steve decided to go out for a walk around the village. I sat in a courtyard with the owner for hours, ultimately seeing everything the factory had on hand. Not one from their production line appealed to me, but I did like various elements of their furniture. Thus, I chose to design something that took an aspect from one chair, another from a different one … and so on. Then I decided to make them even larger than standard chairs. The table base was also unique and large. We agreed on a price and five months later the ensemble arrived in London. They have moved with me to the Algarve in Portugal, to Paris and finally Los Angeles. A friend and I developed a way to add extensions to the glass top and unquestionably, there is not another like it in the world.

Visual art of all kinds became important to me in England. The galleries were unique, with the streets in the West End filled with large and small pieces, some from artists who were well known, most from painters and sculptors who were not, but deserved to be. I went to France and the Louvre and many other galleries in Amsterdam, Belgium, Egypt, large and small. Rubens was, and still is my favorite artist, Cézanne a close second. There are MANY others. In America, Leroy Neiman heads our list. Not too esoteric, but art Carol and I can identify with. Amongst others we have Thomas Pradzynski, Pierre Brisson, Mihail Chemiakin, Joan Miro and Mark Chagall. Of course others not as famous, but they make us smile. There is one I acquired in 1971, from an antique dealer. That's another story for another time. It's of a rose, supposedly painted in the mid 1880's. Valuable perhaps, but I've never had it examined. It represents another era and people I used to know. When the time comes, the children can decide what to do with it and other works. We don't purchase art because of a possible profit later, but only because the work pleases us to live with. Art is so individualistic. It's impossible to please everyone, so we just buy to please ourselves.

In Paris some years back, I walked to the Gallery Magen David on a very narrow cobble stoned street on Rue Le Seine, in Saint-Germain de Prés. It was fairly late and the sky was darkening quickly. I even smelled rain heading in. When I got there, the owner and his wife, whom I had known for years, were very pleased to see me. There was to be an auction that evening! Paintings, sculptures and all sorts of works were to be placed on the block. I noticed a piece for sale that I fell for immediately. It was a sculpture of the head of a woman. She had a smile that melted me. The owners designated it as the first piece to be auctioned. That way, I could bid before all the invitees arrived. Lightning and rain began to hit, and we knew that those coming would be late. The gallery owners started the auction on time. I was one of only a few people there and won her. It wasn't more than ten minutes later that the rain stopped and the room started to fill. As other items were being raised for bids, someone asked about the Greek head. They were politely told it was already sold a bit earlier. Three different people approached me and offered much more than I paid, but I simply said, "Not for sale." I could have made a handsome profit. However, I knew where she would rest in our home in Los Angeles and nowhere else while I was alive. Art is love and never for sale.

You may recall that Carol and I took private houseboats through three different canals in France. A week each, every year, for three consecutive years, with Carol the captain and I the sole crew member. On one cruise we went to Chablis. We moored and rode our onboard bicycles into the town. We noticed a wine tasting at an art gallery. In jeans and T-shirts we pedaled there. It was a marvelous experience. The couple who owned the gallery and Carol and I hit it off from the onset. We drank good Chablis and viewed the art hanging on the walls. There was one piece we liked and they were pleased, as it was from a local artist who was growing in stature. We chatted and bought it. It was late and they were about to close. They invited us to their villa and to dinner. Their cellar housed hundreds of marvelous wines and we sat there at a very old table and sampled some, as they opened them just for us. Later we all went to a local restaurant and were there until it closed. Afterwards they took us, along with our bikes, back to the houseboat. The painting now hangs in our bedroom.

One year in Geneva we saw a long, lovely vase in a window of a gallery. It is somewhat rare as it is made entirely of eggshells, then hand painted. We had it shipped by plane and were pleased to see that they packed it perfectly. We have never seen another.

Trigger, our pony in the dining room, was made by Terrie Read Kvenild in Carmel CA., from hundreds of damaged porcelain ceramic plates that all come from Gumps of San Francisco. They send them to her and she takes months to make an animal from them. Her clients are usually consulates and embassies. Inside is cement and our Trigger weighs about 450 pounds! We needed a small fork lift to get him up here. The base was designed by James Kwan, and made from sapeli, an African wood.

We have quite a few of what I call "things." Bentley, our dear butler in the entrance hall, came from Las Vegas. An aquarium in the bedroom was born when we took out the fireplace. Most of its inhabitants have been with us for years and have names.

A special open face carved in wood was sculpted by a woman who did it when she served in the US Navy. I appreciate one-off's as well as original art, and there are many of these in our home. The art we own is not show and tell. Some pieces may be costly, others not at all, but they are all there for our personal pleasure.

Writing this chapter has made me realize that I've made it a mission to sample a wide variety of artists' works. These are offered to everyone, but I feel immensely pleased to have recognized their value for enhancing one's existence. Art has definitely played an important role in shaping my character and enjoyment of life.

CHERISHED FAMILY AND OTHER PEOPLE WHO HAVE TOUCHED AND HELPED MOLD MY LIFE

First of all, there is my father, who passed away at 44, but who left a wonderful legacy. When he died, a huge group of people from all walks of life attended his funeral. He loved my mother dearly. He taught me so much and was never too busy to be there for Steve and me. He was a man who enjoyed life, valued work, could sing with the best of them, and adored his two sons. A very special person.

My mother was made in heaven just for him. As I've written earlier, she was warm, tender but dignified. She passed on at 81, but in that time taught me much. She passed on her love of books and art. Her openness, acceptance, keen eye for both amusement and people, are gifts that have stayed with me all my life.

In Miami, I had a teacher named Andre Bialinki. He gave out writing assignments every week, fiction and nonfiction. He believed the stringing of words together was imperative if we were to grow intellectually. He and his wife were both writers and loved the experience of writing. I've no idea what it was, except there was something about them I found interesting. They had accents from a country I've long forgotten. But they read my stories at least twice each. They checked, they criticized, they smiled and discussed almost every word on every line with me. I saw they did not do that with anyone else. They asked me to stay after school to discuss writing in general, and lent me books on the subject. I read the works of many well known as well as unheard-of authors that semester. The couple predicted that writing was to be my profession. However, many other factors entered my life and I was not able to fulfill their wishes. But I never forgot them. They had a profound influence on me.

Moving forward in time, I was now in London, producing medical equipment that was unique. However, if I were to succeed I would need to travel to many other countries to market the products. I joined the BHEC, The British Hospital Export Council, for their assistance and guidance. It was there I met my favorite Welshman, Fred Jenkins. I was in my mid 30's, Fred was already in his mid 60's. We went to the same exhibitions and symposia worldwide, and gradually we sort of grew on each other. I certainly was making mistakes, and he saw them. Finally in Tokyo he asked me if I wanted to have dinner with him. I immediately said yes. It turned into one of the most important meals of my life. He asked me a few business questions, and I had no reply to any of them. I simply did not know the answers. He had never become more than a sales manager for a 100 year old company, named Scott & Scott, while I continued to take some tremendous chances and eventually became Chairman, Chief Executive and owner of my own companies. But I knew I had not learned nearly as much as Fred had already forgotten.

From early in our time together, Fred was a mentor, and I had a lot to learn. Whenever we met I probed his mind for answers. I offered him positions in my company, with every perk I could think of. No, he always replied. As he was getting on in years, he explained that to move now would not be fair to Scott & Scott. Then a few months after one of my offers, he surprised me with a phone call to my home. "Do you still want me?" he asked. "Of course!" I replied. "Enough to buy Scott & Scott? I just found out that one of the brothers is retiring and the other would prefer to sell the company than run it himself." I asked how much would it cost and the next morning went to see my bank manager. Within a week I had the funds, took a train to Bournemouth, met Mr. Scott and was the proud owner of a factory that manufactured metal bed pan washers! I made Fred Jenkins a Vice President and Director. That business and my other medical manufacturing business increased many times over. He had a heart attack the next year and died. But

I was always thankful for the friendship and knowledge he provided me.

Speaking of money there was my accountant, Stanley Michaels. We had only been together a few weeks when he paid me a visit in my office. I had just concluded a transaction and was paid in cash. I smiled at Stanley and put the money in my pocket. His face grew red. "Why is that in your pocket? It should be sent to the bank immediately, and declared on your tax form. If not, and if I ever see or hear of this again, you will have to find a new accountant." I went into the bank immediately. Stanley taught me a valuable lesson and was with me for over 25 years.

Lastly, there was Duffy Shoyer. A dear friend, older than I, and indeed a confidant. I was quite unlike the two children he had, a son and daughter who were roughly the same age as I was. Duffy was a very successful restaurateur with a number of fine dining establishments. He married young and regretted it. His son and daughter were in their 20's when we met. They never completed their schooling as he had hoped they would, and were as spoiled as his wife. He had two partners, and one day with holidays coming up, they all decided to go to Europe. Duffy was anxious to see the monuments, the museums, great old landmarks he had only read about. He always had a book in his hands, and was an elegant self-educated gentleman. Alas, when they arrived in each country his partners wanted to see the nightspots, the wild and crazy Europe they had heard about. When they flew back home the partners could not find Duffy at the airport. No, he had discovered that there was a flight returning to Europe shortly after they touched ground. He was on it. He went back and saw all the places and sites he'd missed because his partners were not interested. On his return he sold his one-third share to them. He did well and gave his wife and children funds with these words, "That's it. Make the best of it, as there will be very little left when I'm gone."

Duffy built a villa in Spain, but would visit me in London frequently. We would dine, go to the theater and museums, and he would explain why in his opinion, his life was not all it should have been. He warned me to not make the same mistakes, advising me of all that could and should be in my life. There were times he came, took a back seat in my office and just watched and listened. Those evenings we would meet for dinner and he would on occasion offer a bit of advice. He was always right. I felt as if my father had sent him to guide me, now that he was gone. As he aged, Duffy sold the villa in Spain and moved to Florida. I had moved on to Paris. He called me there at my home and said, "This is it, our last conversation. I've been advised I have not long to live. But I just want to say I wish you were my son, because I love you." He passed away a few days later. I can only hope that if he is looking down, I made him proud.

Please allow Bentley to usher you into the Mintz home

EPILOGUE

Life has taken me down many paths. Some marvelous and others not so pleasant. But I've learned we need to deal with many different situations and times in life. I've visited fifty-five countries and met countless people. I've had some friends who sadly have passed on, who still cross my mind from time to time. I was gifted with a wonderful family and friends that I care for dearly.

We never know how long we have — think of those lost in 9/11; so many young people who will never have the possibilities of doing so many interesting things that life has to offer.

I hope that you who read this book will take the opportunity to experience all you can, and cherish each day, each experience, each person who is close, supports or inspires you in your life. And I hope you kids in our family will do as my father told me to do, and take advantage of the many joys life has to offer.

Alon ... (Rocky)

* * *

Ed. Note ... In the spirit of enjoying life's pleasures, we bring you an example of Alon's idea of a perfect evening at home. According to wife Carol, the couple often invite a small bevy of friends and family for dinner, sometimes a potluck. Menus are posted on a blackboard, and each dish has a tabletop card describing the ingredients.

GOOD EVENING……..

Tonight we have a light dinner, with a pleasant mixture of dishes.

Everything was prepared today using only the freshest of ingredients. After some light appetizers…

There are two platters of wild salmon from Alaska, known as "Carol's Celestial Salmon." The fillets have marinated all day in oils and herbs, French leeks, lemon, crushed Sonoma tomatoes, and a tad of white wine. This dish was first baked, then broiled under a low flame.

We are serving some unusual side dishes tonight. As some patrons do not eat potatoes, there is "Specialité Vegetarian à la Grecque," created with Canadian ratatouille, melded with Napa carrots, a soupçon of garlic and Italian virgin olive oil.

For those who do enjoy potatoes, we have "Cindy's Charm," small Swedish potatoes, baked and then grilled, with red onion and South African diced tomatoes.

As promised, there is also a special dish, "Niki & Taki," stuffed Australian (not hot) peppers, with Japanese crab and pressed Ahi tuna, served with mixed vegetable couscous. The couscous was steamed and then baked, which gives it a black crust, adding to its flavor.

There will be wines from Italy, France, Spain and Portugal served this evening. These will be red wines. However we can uncork a white wine if anyone so desires.

A plate of fresh, mixed goat, cow, ewe and sheep cheeses will conclude the dinner, with possibly a 'tipple' of Greek ouzo or a reserve port.

We hope you will enjoy the evening's dinner and appreciate your patronage!

BON APPÉTIT! ENJOY!

The Management

Alon Mintz

Empty/warmth

The grass is starting to fade on the mountain we shared,
Night is falling a bit earlier over Mill Valley...

You can smell the smoke from more fireplaces now,
I saw three deer prance through the redwoods sunday morn...

The dogs still sleep in the middle of the road,
My beige sweater controls the slight chill in the air...

I must sweep the porch more often now,
The branches are shedding their leaves more rapidly...

It's been so long since I've seen rain in these hills,
I'll wet my face with the first offering...

You don't see as many hitch-hikers now,
Even a hippie wants a winter home thats warm...

Summer is almost gone, and the mini's skirts are fewer in between,
The long gingham maxi's appear more often,..midi ? Never..

I've been conjuring up, and seeking new recipies,
It'll soon be time for warm foods...

The winding rustically treed road leading to my home is the
same, beckoning mysteriously as if to the unknown...

I open the door, the jingle of the bells, the hard wood of
the floor,..the smell of the ash from the night before.....

There can be no question,..I am home.........
where are you...........?

If you liked this book, you might also enjoy these books from Pawpress...

Sensual Spirit…poetry and thoughts from the place where body and soul meet, by Chrystine Julian. "What a rapturous book! Chrystine Julian weds wit and wisdom, body and spirit, in these poems. Her warmth and humor and deep insight radiate off every page." *Gayle Brandeis, author of "Fruitflesh, Seeds of Inspiration for Women that Write," "Self Storage" and the Bellwether Prize winner, "The Book of Dead Birds."*

Pawprints by Ina Hillebrandt, Amazon.com top seller featured on ABC Nightly News, PBS, etc. From "Moonlit Fox" to "Nose Fur," more than 100 short, short "tails" of close encounters of the furry kind. Uplifts, inspires readers to write, and promotes kindness to animals. Purr-fect gift for animal lovers and pets of all ages. "The stories make you feel you are right there…I love them!" Teresa Proscewitz, Chief Forester, City of LA Dept. of Recreation and Parks. ISBN 1-880882-01-9.

The Student Prints, Educators' Guide to Pawprints Literacy Plus™ —The Innovative Standards-Based Literacy and Environmental Program. © 2001 Ina S. Hillebrandt. Companion curriculum guide to *Pawprints,* developed following Pawprints Literacy Plus training module for Jane Goodall Institute. For teachers and parents, grades 1-8, and ESL. "*Pawprints* is a new form of great literature...the book and these exercises have the power to change the way kids…and…adults think." Maxwell Yerger, Reading Specialist/Teacher/Trainer, NY, NY. ISBN 1-880882–03-5.

How to Write Your Memoirs — Fun Prompts to Make Writing … and Reading …Your Life Stories a Pleasure! by Ina Hillebrandt. Easy steps and prompts to make organizing those scraps of paper — physical and mental — fun and rewarding, for the writer, family and friends, and possibly, the public! ISBN 1-880882-04-3. "The questions make it easy!" *Gertrude Brucker, Member, Felicia Mahood Senior Center, Los Angeles*

Stories From The Heart, Volumes 1-3 … Selected stories to delight and inspire readers to create their own memoirs and fiction. Vol. 3 Includes writing tools and carefully selected memoirs — and fiction! — to entertain, and help readers craft their own enchanting life histories. *"Multi-hued, textured tales – from such stuff was woven the*

American Dream." Marvin J. Wolf, Author of Fallen Angels and many other nonfiction books.

Vol. 2, From great grape fiascos to wars…Wit and wisdom by the Pawprints Writing Club (now Footprints) became an **Amazon.com top seller**. Poignant, funny, tender, frightening, insightful memories of the holocaust, flying a plane, bees, first love, South Africa, India in the time of the Raj, cookies and much more. *"The section I most enjoyed was a few punning stories about cats by the late Earl Boretz...most amusing. His characters include Count Fe-Line the cat burglar in Pussy footin' around; Sinister, the three-legged pirate cat and Sorrowful, the witch...Overall, an entertaining collection." Cecilia Blight, Nelm News, newsletter of The **National English Literary Museum**, Grahamstown, S. Africa.*

Vol. 1 features the first delightful tails by Earl Boretz, plus the special whimsy of Arabella Bel-Mitchell, a British lady with an outrageous sense of humor and fantasy, along with lyrical and heartfelt memoirs by authors from various walks of life.

All three ***Stories*** books compiled and edited by Ina Hillebrandt. Vol. 1 ISBN. 1-880882-07-8. Vol. 2 ISBN 1-880882-08-6 Vol. 3 ISBN 1-80882-04-3.

Go East, Young Man, Go East! *Memoirs of an eyewitness to the oil boom and culture clashes of the Middle East.* By Charles Alan Tichenor, Edited by Ina Hillebrandt. A book of memoirs penned by a witty and informed hand, with tales of political intrigue, spies, cultural exchanges and the effects of black gold on royalty and desert-dwelling Bedouins. ISBN 1-880882-09-4.

Published by Angel Fire Publications

The Angel Chronicles, *by J.K. Johnson.* A compelling murder mystery/ romance with feet in this world and another plane. Written originally from behind prison bars, this page turner by a multi-talented woman inspires readers to say, "It's a life changer! And a great read." ISBN 978-0-9819193-0-0.

www.ingramcontent.com/pod-product-compliance
Lightning Source LLC
Chambersburg PA
CBHW060255100426
42742CB00011B/1756
9781880882146